WIS
G

GUY KAWASAKI

with **MADISUN NUISMER**

WISER GUY

Life-Changing Revelations
and Revisions *from*
TECH'S CHIEF EVANGELIST

WILEY

Copyright © 2025 by John Wiley & Sons, Inc. All rights reserved, including rights for text and data mining and training of artificial technologies or similar technologies.

Published by John Wiley & Sons, Inc., Hoboken, New Jersey.
Published simultaneously in Canada.

No part of this publication may be reproduced, stored in a retrieval system, or transmitted in any form or by any means, electronic, mechanical, photocopying, recording, scanning, or otherwise, except as permitted under Section 107 or 108 of the 1976 United States Copyright Act, without either the prior written permission of the Publisher, or authorization through payment of the appropriate per-copy fee to the Copyright Clearance Center, Inc., 222 Rosewood Drive, Danvers, MA 01923, (978) 750-8400, fax (978) 750-4470, or on the web at www.copyright.com. Requests to the Publisher for permission should be addressed to the Permissions Department, John Wiley & Sons, Inc., 111 River Street, Hoboken, NJ 07030, (201) 748-6011, fax (201) 748-6008, or online at http://www.wiley.com/go/permission.

The manufacturer's authorized representative according to the EU General Product Safety Regulation is Wiley-VCH GmbH, Boschstr. 12, 69469 Weinheim, Germany, e-mail: Product_Safety@wiley.com.

Trademarks: Wiley and the Wiley logo are trademarks or registered trademarks of John Wiley & Sons, Inc. and/or its affiliates in the United States and other countries and may not be used without written permission. All other trademarks are the property of their respective owners. John Wiley & Sons, Inc. is not associated with any product or vendor mentioned in this book.

Limit of Liability/Disclaimer of Warranty: While the publisher and author have used their best efforts in preparing this book, they make no representations or warranties with respect to the accuracy or completeness of the contents of this book and specifically disclaim any implied warranties of merchantability or fitness for a particular purpose. No warranty may be created or extended by sales representatives or written sales materials. The advice and strategies contained herein may not be suitable for your situation. You should consult with a professional where appropriate. Further, readers should be aware that websites listed in this work may have changed or disappeared between when this work was written and when it is read. Neither the publisher nor authors shall be liable for any loss of profit or any other commercial damages, including but not limited to special, incidental, consequential, or other damages.

For general information on our other products and services or for technical support, please contact our Customer Care Department within the United States at (800) 762-2974, outside the United States at (317) 572-3993 or fax (317) 572-4002.

Wiley also publishes its books in a variety of electronic formats. Some content that appears in print may not be available in electronic formats. For more information about Wiley products, visit our web site at www.wiley.com.

Library of Congress Cataloging-in-Publication Data is Available:

ISBN: 9781394324828 (Cloth)
ISBN: 9781394324835 (ePub)
ISBN: 9781394324842 (ePDF)

Cover Design: Wiley
Cover Image: © Nina/stock.adobe.com. Generated with AI
Author Photos: Guy Kawasaki @ Liz DePuydt, Madisun Nuismer @ Danny Witty

SKY10119377_062025

To Beth, Nic, Sakura, Duke, Noah, Lauren, Nohemi, Anthony, and Nate

Wisdom is the power to put our time and our knowledge to the proper use.

—Thomas J. Watson Jr.

Contents

Preface		*xi*
Mahalo		*xiii*
Chapter 1	Foundation	1
Chapter 2	Motivation	17
Chapter 3	Inspiration	29
Chapter 4	Realization	45
Chapter 5	Exhortation	63
Chapter 6	Observation	87
Chapter 7	Innovation	115
Chapter 8	Salvation	133
Chapter 9	Joculation	153
Chapter 10	Validation	165
Summation		*187*
About the Authors		*191*
Index		*193*

Preface

> The only true wisdom is in knowing you know nothing.
>
> —Socrates

Before you ask or wonder, this is not my autobiography or memoir. It is a compilation of the most enlightening stories of my life—mostly ones I've lived but some that I've heard. Think personal lessons, not personal history.

This book started as a simple project: Get back the rights of *Wise Guy* from Penguin, make a few edits, get a new cover, and push it out. That's not what happened. Think complete restoration as opposed to simple detailing.

It's how I roll—or, as Madisun says, "You always need a project, Guy."

My stories do not depict epic, tragic, or heroic occurrences because this wasn't the trajectory of my life. They do not depict a rapid, tech-bro rise, either. One decision. One failure. Hard work. One success. My goal is to educate, not awe you.

There are, however, stories that depict epic, tragic, and heroic occurrences. I was blessed to learn these because of my podcast,

Remarkable People. Without a doubt, these stories made me a wiser Guy.

I hope our book will help you live a joyous, productive, and remarkable life. If *Wiser Guy* succeeds at this, that's the best story of all.

—Guy Kawasaki
Santa Cruz, California, 2025

Mahalo

Feeling gratitude and not expressing it is like wrapping a present and not giving it.

—William Arthur Ward

Mahalo is the Hawaiian word for "thank you," but its emotional impact is greater than a quick-and-dirty "thanks." When coming from a person with ties to Hawaii, it's a term to express deep, heartfelt appreciation.

So this is my chance to thank the people who've shaped my journey, supported my work, and made this book possible. Writing about the stories that made me wise was a deeply personal endeavor, and I couldn't have done it without them.

First, my family. My wife, Beth, is my rock, my editor, and my reality check. She's been my partner, and her love and patience have been the foundation of my life. To my kids, Nic, Noah, Nohemi, and Nate—you've taught me more about life, love, and resilience than any job or deal ever could. And Will Mayall, whom I consider the brother I never had. You are my greatest teachers.

xiv Mahalo

Second, the *Remarkable People* podcast team—Madisun Nuismer, Jeff Sieh, Tessa Nuismer, and Shannon Hernandez—and incredible guests, such as Jane Goodall, Stephen Wolfram, Bob Cialdini, Halim Flowers, Katy Milkman, Marylène Delbourg-Delphis, Carol Dweck, and Angela Duckworth. They shared their wisdom and trusted me with their stories.

Third, the Yakookza cabal of catty surf buddies. ("Yakookza" is my made-up word combining *yakuza* and kook—you can figure this out.) Their names are Mark Nishimura, Cynthea Williford, John Conway, Joanna Mana, and Troy Obrero. FIIG!

Fourth, my editors, past and present: Rick Kot and Leah Zarra plus the teams behind them at Penguin and Wiley. Thank you for your patience, vision, and ability to turn my ramblings into something coherent. You've been a true partner in this process.

Fifth, my colleagues from Apple, especially Mike Boich, Joanna Hoffman, Alain Rossmann, Mike Murray, Steve Jobs, Carol Ballard, and Holly Lory. You taught me the art of thinking differently. The lessons I learned during those years have shaped my career and my approach to life.

Sixth, my readers and listeners. Your support means the world to me, and I write and podcast for you. You've allowed me to share my ideas, my failures, and my successes, and for that I'm eternally grateful.

Seventh, to the people who've doubted me, robbed me, or gave me a ride in a Porsche or Ferrari. You've been some of my greatest motivators. Every "no can do" has pushed me to find a better way, and every setback has made me wiser. And every car ride motivated me with envy.

Finally, Madisun Nuismer. Yes, she was mentioned before, but she is what's known as a "force multiplier," not to mention producer and co-author, so she deserves two *mahalo* mentions.

You would be surprised to learn how much of my compassion, efficiency, and effectiveness is because of her.

Wiser Guy is the culmination of a lifetime of lessons, and it's dedicated to everyone who's been part of my journey. Thank you for making me wiser. I hope this book does the same for you.

1 | Foundation

> You don't have to be great to start, but you have to start to be great.
>
> —Zig Ziglar

Foundation: the basis or groundwork of anything.

My Draft-Dodging Humble Heritage

My family emigrated to Hawaii from Japan between 1890 and 1900. At the time Japan was fighting in two major conflicts: the First Sino-Japanese War and the Russ-Japanese War.

Young Japanese men were required to serve in the military, so my family immigrated to Hawaii and worked as sugar cane laborers. It is safer, after all, to harvest sugar in Hawaii for $1/day than to invade China or Russia. Also, my great-grandfather was on the FBI watch list because he traveled to Japan under two different names.

My father started working at age fourteen to support the family. He graduated from high school but did not get a college degree. He became a stevedore, then a fireman, and finally a real estate agent. His deep sense of civic duty led him into politics, and he was a state senator for approximately twenty years.

Like my father, my mother did not attend college. Her family, however, was well off, so she went to Yokohama, Japan, in 1939 for schooling. Fortunately, she returned to Hawaii on one of the last two ships before the Japanese attack on Pearl Harbor in 1941. My mother dedicated her life to our family.

Wisdom

As the saying goes, you have to wait a long time by the side of a river before a roast duck will fly into your mouth. So take charge and be proactive because to win in life, you can't be passive.

The move to Hawaii changed the arc of my family's life, steering us clear of the draft, conventional life in Japan, and the perils of Hiroshima during WWII.

I'm a fortunate and appreciative product of my family's courageous decisions and relentless pursuit of a better future. My family and I owe everything to America.

Thank God for My Sixth-Grade Teacher

I grew up in Kalihi Valley, a low-income part of Honolulu. If you've driven from Honolulu International Airport to Kaneohe via the Wilson Tunnel, you passed right by my boyhood home. At the time, the area was populated by working-class Hawaiians, Filipinos, Samoans, Japanese, and Chinese.

There were few Caucasians, whom locals derogatorily referred to as "haoles." Our neighbors worked as clerks, janitors, and laborers—if they worked at all. Our home was near a public housing project. I didn't venture into it because the majority of the residents were Hawaiians and Samoans, and you only went there if you had to.

I attended a public school called Kalihi Elementary which is housed in the pink buildings on the Ewa (west) side of Likelike Highway. My educational route would have led me from Kalihi Elementary to Kalakaua Middle School, Farrington High School, and the University of Hawaii. After college, I would have worked in a retail, tourism, or agricultural job.

However, it was not my destiny because my sixth-grade schoolteacher, Trudy Akau, advised my parents to take me out of the public school system and get me into a private, college-prep school—specifically, Punahou or Iolani.

Akau's advice changed the course of my life. If she had not persuaded my parents to send me to Iolani and if my parents hadn't made the necessary sacrifices to pay Iolani's tuition, I would not have gone to Stanford. If I had not gone to Stanford, I would not have met the guy who piqued interested in computers and hired me at Apple.

Wisdom

First, become a Trudy Akau. Take interest in others, help them, get beyond your comfort zone, and offer guidance to them and their families. One caring person altered the trajectory of my life. You could do the same.

Foundation 5

Second, follow the advice of people like Trudy Akau. Teachers, coaches, counselors, and ministers are motivated by a desire to help others. They typically have your best interests at heart. Pay attention to what they say.

Third, before it's too late, express gratitude to the Trudy Akaus in your life. Not thanking her is one of my biggest regrets.

If you are a teacher, coach, pastor, priest, or rabbi, or hold a position that influences people, understand that you are, in the words of Steve Jobs, "denting the universe." You may affect only one person at a time and a few over your lifetime, but every dent counts.

Make no mistake: You are doing God's work.

The World Isn't Black and White

As far back as I can remember, my parents instilled a sense of honesty and honor in me. I learned that it was disgraceful to lie, cheat, or steal. One day, when I was a teenager, my uncle challenged this belief system by taking me shopping at the now-defunct Wigwam department store to purchase some screws for his house repair.

He opened a plastic container in the store, took a few screws, and then we left. My uncle was a shoplifter, and I was his accomplice! He justified his actions by saying he only needed a few screws. Even today, at seventy, I still struggle to make sense of why he stole those screws.

Wisdom

First, people aren't simply good or bad. Good people can do bad things, and bad people can do good things. This includes yourself—you will do bad things that you will regret.

Second, remember that you are influencing people who are watching you. The transgression that you consider inconsequential could shape the values and morals of others without you ever knowing it—but so could your kindness and generosity.

6 Wiser Guy

I am sure that if my uncle was aware of the impact this small act would have on me, he would have purchased the full container of screws.

A Little Fear Is Good

Three other youthful experiences taught me to respect grown-ups and not screw around. The first occurred on a Kalihi Elementary field trip to the Nike (nothing to do with the shoe company) missile site in Kahuku, Hawaii.

Following the tour, the Army served us lunch, and I dropped a clump of rice on the floor. I picked it up and was about to throw it back on the floor when an Army officer, speaking in an frightening, authoritative, drill sergeant tone, said, "Don't throw anything on the floor. Pick it up and bus your tray." He scared the crap out of me, and ever since then I've respected those in uniform and accepted the responsibility to keep things clean.

The second formative experience occurred when my father took me to his workplace, the alarm bureau of the Honolulu Fire Department. This facility dispatched fire trucks when people reported a fire.

While waiting for him one day after school, I set off an alarm box to see what would happen. I wasn't aware that the box was there for demonstration purposes. My father convinced me that I had caused firemen to jump down the pole into a firetruck and rush to the scene.

He also informed me that it was a crime to make a false alarm. Therefore, the police might come after me. He and his buddies had a good laugh, but the experience turned me into a scaredy-cat who didn't break the law. This lesson probably kept me out of much teenage-boy, reptilian-brain trouble.

The third experience occurred at Iolani. The only time that I got into trouble in high school was when I recruited a buddy

Foundation

to skip art class with me. Stupidly, we chose the same day when a few other students did the same thing.

We received a detention, and in my case the punishment was sweeping the basketball gym floor for a week. This experience didn't scare me, but it taught me an valuable lesson because it was embarrassing. And I hate being embarrassed.

My parents also gave me hell for doing this. After all, they were making a big investment in my education. Back then, there weren't many doting helicopter parents (the ones that "hover" over their kids to protect them).

Teachers were always right, and you did what they said. End of discussion. This sounds antiquated now, but the "teacher as all-powerful" approach worked for me.

Wisdom

There are two ways to learn from these experiences. First, teach others to respect authority. Contrary to the popular belief that one must always be supportive, nurturing, and protective, scaring people can be a good thing too. Sometimes you should just listen and obey, rather than question and debate.

Second, learn from people in authority. You cannot do anything you want to and always get away with it. And not getting away with some things is an exceptionally good lesson in how the world works.

The Toughest Teachers Are the Best

Think about the best teachers you had in your life—regardless of when or where. Go to that place in your mind, and you'll get the full impact of what I'm about to tell you.

At the age of fourteen, I started the seventh grade at Iolani. This was a private, Episcopalian, college-prep school that offered instruction from kindergarten to twelfth grade. When I

8   Wiser Guy

attended, it was an all-boys school with a graduating class of 150 pupils.

Iolani was an excellent experience. Among the Iolani teachers and staff, Harold Keables had the most influence on me. He was my Advanced Placement English teacher—and the toughest teacher I've ever had at any level of school.

He taught me how to hold myself to high standards and the value of hard work. For example, here's how he taught writing:

> He highlighted the errors that you made.
>
> You copied the sentence as you originally wrote it.
>
> You cited and quoted the rule that you violated from *Good Writing: An Informal Manual of Style* by Alan Vrooman.
>
> You rewrote the sentence correctly.
>
> You submitted this as homework and hoped you got it right the second time.

This was the 1970s—long before personal computers and word processing—so we wrote everything out in cursive with a pen. When each error required three steps to rectify, you learned the rules of grammar and spelling after a few papers. Keables is the reason I disdain the passive voice and adore the serial comma.

I eventually read *The Chicago Manual of Style* from cover to cover because Keables inspired such meticulous attention to detail. I hope that you are taught by a Harold Keables at least once in your life.

Wisdom

First, seek out and embrace people who will challenge you. You will learn more from them than from those who hold you to lower standards. Years later, you'll realize that the toughest

Foundation 9

teachers and bosses were the ones who taught you the most. Iron sharpens iron.

Second, be a hardass if you are a teacher, manager, coach, or someone who has the ability to influence others. Lowering standards and expectations in an effort to be kind, gentle, or popular benefits no one. However, you can do both, which is excellent. The future cost of low standards can be great.

Third, have patience. I wasn't one of Keable's best students, so he's probably now in Heaven, shocked that I'm the one who has written seventeen books. As a teacher, you never know which student will take what you taught and run with it.

Finally, as I advised regarding Trudy Akau, thank those who helped you achieve your goals before they are gone. You'll regret not doing so if the opportunity passes.

Father Knows Best (and Pays the Tuition)

Dan Feldhaus, the college counselor at Iolani, persuaded me to apply to Stanford. My grade point average was 3.4, and my SAT scores were 610 for math and 680 for English. Back then these were good scores, but not great.

No tutors helped me raise my grade point average, and no consultants helped me polish my essays. I did not visit any institutions to get on the radar of the admissions office (even the University of Hawaii, which is a mile from Iolani).

To my surprise, I was accepted. The only explanation is that in the early 1970s, Asian Americans were considered an oppressed minority, therefore my race helped me to get admitted. This was so long ago that discrimination hadn't been reversed for Asians yet!

The University of Hawaii, Occidental, and Stanford all admitted me. (I applied to additional colleges, but I can't recall which ones!) I loved playing football and could have played at

10 Wiser Guy

Occidental, so my first choice was the school that Barack Obama made famous. (Factoid: He supposedly got a B in the politics class of Professor Robert Boesche.)

But my father made the decision for me: "If I'm going to pay all this money, you're going to Stanford. Or you can go to UH (University of Hawaii) for free. I'm not paying for a school so you can play football."

So much for fostering independent thinking in your children. I went to Stanford, and the rest is history.

Wisdom

First, don't allow others to make mistakes. At least play the devil's advocate and explain why they might be making one. Caring is scaring.

My father was right to coerce me into attending Stanford. There were solid reasons for attending Occidental but playing football was not one of them.

Second, acknowledge that others (even your parents!) may be correct even when you are certain they are wrong. You never know . . . and only time can tell.

The Promised Land

Iolani was the first educational institution that transformed my life. Stanford ranks second. That experience began in the fall of 1972, when I stepped off a Western Airlines flight from Honolulu, jumped into a van for incoming freshmen, and rode to the Stanford campus for the first time.

I had no idea what to expect when the van stopped, but I learned fast. California was the Promised Land: exotic cars, blonde beauties, and high-paying tech companies. The skies parted, and the angels sang. This was where God had wanted me to be.

Foundation 11

Stanford broadened my horizons and elevated my aspirations beyond Hawaii's expectations of a job in retailing, tourism, or agriculture. If I hadn't left Hawaii, my life would have turned out quite differently, and I would not have accomplished all that I have.

Mike Boich, the first software evangelist of Apple's Macintosh Division, and I met at Stanford. We were then both sophomores at the time, and we hit it off immediately because of a shared love of cars.

Ten years later, Boich hired me at Apple, and that's how my technology career kicked into high gear.

Wisdom

First, see the world. Get out of your hometown. Embrace the unknown and resist the known. Going to college across the Pacific Ocean—2,336 miles away—was a horizon-expanding, exciting, and fun experience that taught me many important lessons.

Second, even if you excelled at Podunk High, there is always someone who is smarter, bigger, or faster than you. Be ready for this realization to occur, so you aren't destroyed by it.

Third, if you eliminate the outliers who are smarter, bigger, and faster than you, that doesn't mean you can't be better than they are. Maybe you'll just be in the right place at the right time. Or you can outhustle and outwork them because you had to compensate for your shortcomings.

My First Two Career Decisions

If you were an Asian American (or Jewish) kid in the 1970s, your parents hoped you would become a dentist, doctor, or lawyer. There are many ways that your path becomes clear. Let me explain mine.

I went on rounds at the Stanford Medical Center because I had delusions of becoming a doctor. I fainted on the first day, and I interpreted this as a sign that I wasn't meant to be a doctor. I doubt I would have passed organic chemistry anyway.

After my fainting episode at the Stanford Medical Center, medicine was out for me. And I didn't want to spend my life sticking my hands in people's mouths, so dentistry was out as well.

There was only law left. This career path made sense because my father, who didn't attend college, served as a state senator in Hawaii. He encouraged me to pursue a law degree—each generation making progress and all. I applied to law school at Stanford, UC Berkeley, and UC Davis, and I got into UC Davis.

In the fall of 1976, I entered law school. Davis is a small city located just west of Sacramento. It had a population of 36,000 people in 1980, and it was even smaller when I was there. The school is best known for its agriculture and veterinary curriculum.

A classmate from Iolani named Russell Kato had been accepted at the same time, and we shared an apartment. During orientation week, one of the deans told us that although we were bright, we didn't know anything, and law school was going to remake our minds.

If his goal was to intimidate us, he was too effective with me. The law school case-study method involved the professors calling on students and ripping them to pieces. (Remember how the Harvard Law School professor played by John Houseman humiliates his students in the film *The Paper Chase?*)

I didn't even complete the orientation program. I left Russell without a roommate, and I regret that to this day. I also felt that I had failed my parents, who had worked so hard and sacrificed so much so that I could attend college and law school.

Foundation 13

When I told them my decision, I was afraid that they would be furious—perhaps even disown me. My father surprised me by saying, "It's okay . . . as long as you make something of yourself by the time you're twenty-five or so. Just don't waste your life."

I never felt closer to my father than at that moment. Four decades later, my assessment of quitting law school is that it demonstrated self-awareness; many people practice law for twenty years before realizing that they don't want to be lawyers. I came to the same conclusion in just a week.

Wisdom

When I fainted at the Stanford Medical Center, I quickly realized that becoming a doctor was not in my future. And my brief time in law school taught me more about self-awareness than any case study could.

First, trust your instincts when something doesn't feel right. It's like seeing a flashing red light at an intersection: The universe is telling you something.

Second, understand that quitting can be the brave decision, and it doesn't necessarily make you a "quitter." Fears that an action like this leads to a slippery slope that makes you a permanent loser are overblown.

Third, if you're a parent, understand that having control of your kids is an illusion. Yes, scaring is caring, but ultimately your children find their own path.

Tony the Public Health Tiger

One last story about the influence of foundations in life—again, a story about parents and schooling. When I interviewed Dr. Tony Fauci, former director of the National Institute of

14 Wiser Guy

Allergy and Infectious Diseases and advisor to seven US presidents, about his upbringing, he told me this:

> From the time I was a child old enough to remember, my father—this is back in the 1940s and 1950s—was the neighborhood pharmacist, he owned a pharmacy.
>
> Back then the pharmacists are unlike now with the chain drugstores of CVS and Walgreens, which are somewhat very businesslike and impersonal. Whereas he was kind of like the neighborhood psychiatrist, the neighborhood doctor, the neighborhood counselor, and he cared very much about the community.
>
> So from the time I was able to understand things and reach the age of reason, I saw my family devoted to service to the community. And that really laid the foundation for me going into medicine and ultimately going into the public service concept of medicine.
>
> So they had a very, very strong influence on me, as did my schooling. I went to a Jesuit high school, a Jesuit college, and in those environments, the theme of my educational institutions was service to others. And that's been the prevailing theme of my professional life.

Wisdom

Here are two key lessons from Tony's story. First, early role models, particularly parents, shape one's values and career path.

Tony witnessed his father's dedication to community service through his pharmacy work. This early exposure to service-oriented work laid the foundation for his own career choices in medicine and public health.

Foundation 15

Second, educational environments and their core values are also a source of lifelong values. The Jesuit emphasis on "service to others" during Tony formative years reinforced the lessons he learned at home.

This shows how aligned messages between home and school can create a powerful foundation for one's life philosophy and career choices. The consistency between his family's values and his school's teachings created a clear moral compass that guided his future path.

2 | Motivation

Success usually comes to those who are too busy to be looking for it.

— Henry David Thoreau

Motivation: the reason or reasons one has for acting or behaving in a particular way.

Forget the World, Change the Car

From the outside looking in, or the present looking back, you may attribute the motivation of remarkable people to making a difference, saving the planet, or to creating astounding works of art, music, and writing.

More power to you if this is true in your life, but don't feel alone if you have less lofty goals. When I was growing up in Hawaii my family drove a Toyota Corona. It was slow, clunky, and poorly made. I despised even being seen in it.

Around that time, someone offered me a ride in his Porsche 911. I can still vividly recall its awesome lime green color. Then in college, a classmate's father gave me a ride in his Ferrari 275 GT. And Mike Boich's (my college classmate and the guy who gave me a job at Apple) mother asked me to drive her home in her Ferrari Daytona when I visited him in Phoenix.

This was the same day that Mike's father picked us up from the Phoenix airport in a Rolls Royce. Riding in a Rolls and driving a Ferrari in the same day was a mind- and motivation-expanding experience for a boy from a low-income part of Honolulu.

I didn't care about changing the world at the time. I just wanted to change the car and this is what spurred me to study hard and work hard.

Wisdom

Motivation comes in many forms, and there's no need to apologize if yours isn't just about preserving the earth. For me, it was as simple as upgrading from a Toyota Corona—a tangible prospect that fueled my grit and ambition.

Let your desires—even the seemingly materialistic ones—drive you to achieve remarkable things. Don't worry about what motivates you. What's important is that you are motivated and complete the assignment.

Because of the profound impact these experiences had on me, I now let my children, their friends, and other young people ride in and drive my cars.

Woz Explains What Motivated Steve Jobs

Successful companies get to rewrite their past, so you might think that Steve Jobs and Steve Wozniak in the proverbial garage in Cupertino, California, were all about democratizing computers for "the rest of us."

Again, we are encountering that pesky concept of lofty ideals and motivations. However, this is how Steve Wozniak explained the formation of Apple to me:

> His [Steve Jobs's] idea was not a computer company. His idea was what he knew. He'd sold surplus electronic parts. He knew how to buy switches and capacitors and transistors and sell them, and even some little low-level chips . . .
>
> He wanted to start out and just make a PC board that would cost us twenty bucks a board to build, and we'd sell them for forty bucks. Neither one of us could really come up with a good argument that we'd make money, but he said, "Well, at least for once in our life, we'd have a company."
>
> One thing he wanted was to somehow be important in the world, and he didn't have the academic background or really business background, but he had at least me, and so he said, "Let's start a company."

Wisdom

I will say it again: "Don't sweat the source of your motivation." Just get motivated somehow and then pay the price. Be the success who got motivated by whatever silly, insipid, or dire circumstance did the trick.

Motivation 21

Steve Jobs simply wanted to be a big deal. I wanted a nice car. Those kinds of ambitions paid off for us, and they can pay off for you.

Crime Can Pay

I was a victim of crime twice in high school. In both instances, a "moke" stole money from me. "Moke" is the Hawaiian word for a delinquent, criminal, or tough guy, usually of Hawaiian or Pacific-Island ancestry. It rhymes with "stoke" and "bloke" but not "poke," the raw-fish dish that rhymes with "okay."

The first crime occurred at a bus stop in front of Kaimuki High School, a public school across the street from Iolani. As I waited for a bus to go home, a big moke approached me and demanded money. I lost a few dollars—and my self-esteem.

The second crime took place in front of Farrington High School, three miles from my house in Kalihi Valley. Another moke demanded money from me as I sat on a public bus.

He was smaller than the moke in the first story but menacing nonetheless. The total take was again a few dollars plus my self-esteem. More than forty years later, I would recognize this guy if I ever saw him.

My experiences were mild compared to what many children go through, and I was not in serious physical danger. But they were scary for me. I despised the fear and intimidation that I felt. To this day I avoid public transportation, and I consider myself a coward for not fighting back.

Wisdom

Make unpleasant experiences into something positive. Being robbed, even in a modest way, inspired me to study in school and work hard after graduation because I never wanted to ride a bus again and didn't want to live in a high-crime neighborhood.

Wiser Guy

I don't promote robbery as a source of motivation, nor do I hope it befalls any of you, but it did inspire me to study and work hard.

"Are You Jackie Chan?"

Circa 1990. I was at a stoplight on El Camino Real in Menlo Park, California, driving a Porsche 911 when I noticed a car to my left with four teenage girls in it. They smiled, giggled, and made eye contact with me.

Smugness ensued.

These girls must have recognized me for a variety of reasons: my work at Apple, my books, my talks, my hot startup, or maybe (wishful thinking) my looks. In any case, I thought I had arrived: even teenage girls knew who I was.

The girl in the front passenger seat signaled for me to roll down my window, and as the affable person that I am, I did. She then leaned out of her window and asked, "Are you Jackie Chan?" All I could do was shake my head and laugh. So much for fame. I was just an Asian who resembled a *renowned* Asian.

Since that day, one of my goals has been for Jackie Chan to look over from his Bentley at a stoplight, see a car full of teenage girls trying to make eye contact with him, and for one of them to motion for him to roll down his window, at which point she will ask, "Are you Guy Kawasaki?"

Wisdom

Do not flatter yourself. We're all specks of dust in the universe. My speck happens to resemble Jackie Chan. However, for the umpteenth time, it doesn't matter what motivates you as long as you're motivated, so Jackie, I'm coming for you . . .

$250,000 in Checking

Sandy Kurtzig earned a math degree from UCLA in 1968, and went on to be one of the few female engineering students at Stanford. After earning her aeronautical engineering master's degree, Kurtzig went to work for General Electric, where she sold computer timesharing.

She left this position to launch Ask Group in a spare bedroom. It developed software to manage manufacturing. In 1981, she was the first woman to take a Silicon Valley tech company public. Kurtzig's share of the company was worth $67 million at the time.

Sometime in the mid-1980s, Sandra and I met through my evangelism job at Apple. At one point, she was having trouble with her Macintosh, so I went to her house to provide tech support.

When I sat down to work on her Macintosh, I saw that she was running Quicken, a checkbook program. Its window was front and center on the screen. I was familiar with Quicken, so I knew exactly where to look for the current balance, and I couldn't help but do so.

She had $250,000 in her checking account (almost $750,000 in 2025 dollars). I was blown away. I walked out of her house with a new benchmark: to someday have at least $250,000 in my checking account.

Wisdom

Embrace the inspiration of people's success. I didn't begrudge Kurtzig her wealth. Quite the contrary—her checkbook balance showed me what a hard-working entrepreneur could achieve. Until then, I was usually content if my bank balance wasn't negative.

However, you can usually ignore people who inherited their wealth. They often did little beyond winning the birth lottery.

No One Complained About Me?

In July 2018, a Santa Cruz surfing instructor was working with my kids and me. He had a serious talk with my daughter Nohemi and son Nate after receiving complaints that they were catching too many waves. They asked him to tell Nohemi and Nate to catch fewer waves.

Three questions immediately popped into my mind: First, was it my kids' fault that they are good? Second, was it the instructor's fault that he coached them so well they were successful? Third, was it my kids' or the instructor's responsibility that the complainers weren't able to catch as many waves?

That said, there is a code and etiquette that people share waves and not take too many. The instructor did talk to my kids because you are supposed to catch a wave and then wait your turn.

Later, I asked him if anyone had complained that *I* caught too many waves, and the answer was "No, no one mentioned you," which deeply upset me.

As a result, it became a source of motivation for me to become so competent that others would complain about me catching too many waves too.

Wisdom

There is a lesson for complainers here: get better. Instead of whining because two kids are getting more waves than you, get motivated to get better by siting in the right place, picking the right wave, paddling harder, and using the right kind of surfboard.

Motivation 25

If my kids had complained that they weren't getting enough waves, I would have told them to suck it up and get better. And the fact that no one complained about me catching too many waves fueled my desire to be the someone people complained about.

Shut Down Your Nigel

One of the most powerful sources of negativity is your own mind. Julia Cameron, the queen of creativity and author of more than forty books including *The Artist's Way*, has an imaginary buddy and inner critic she calls Nigel.

According to Julia, Nigel is a gay British interior designer for whom nothing she produces is good enough. To quote Julia:

> I do the morning writing every day, and Nigel says, "Oh, you're boring," and you say, "Thank you for sharing, Nigel," and you just keep on writing. What happens is that your Nigel, your critic, becomes miniaturized. It becomes a cartoon voice, and not something deadly, forbidding, looming, and frightening.

If the queen of creativity has to shut down her inner demotivator, we probably all do! It may seem trite, but naming your inner critic is beneficial because it compartmentalizes doubt into a single entity. The relationship can become amusing and lighthearted—and most likely more constructive.

Wisdom

Face your inner critic head-on. It is an important step toward creativity and success. Julia demonstrates how lowering that critical voice to a manageable size, such as turning Nigel into a

26 Wiser Guy

harmless cartoon, allows us to keep writing, innovating, and pushing boundaries.

By naming and engaging with your inner critic, you turn doubt and cynicism into motivation—even Julia's got a Nigel, and she's doing awesome.

Off-the-Books Learning

When I interviewed Joe Foster, the founder of Reebok, I learned that he and his brother went to college to learn about the shoe business even though they were third-generation shoemakers. I'll let him explain the "off-the-books" benefits that he gained.

> Obviously working at the family business, we knew how to make football boots, rugby boots, soccer boots, whatever.
>
> But we became friends with a lot of people who knew the answers to a lot of questions. Where do we get this machine from? Where do we get this material from? How do we do this? What are different techniques?

Wisdom

This story illustrates the depth and complexity of real-world motivation. In this case, there were other reasons to go to college besides getting a degree, such as industry connections with experts and peers and complementary knowledge derived outside of their hands-on experience in the shoe industry.

So if you are fortunate enough to go to school, get everything you can out of the experience—not just the degrees, but the connections and real-world knowledge that may prove valuable.

Motivation 27

From Twelfth to Gold

One last story about motivation. Kristi Yamaguchi told me that she placed twelfth in her first figure skating competition. She asked her mother why the girls in first, second, and third place got ribbons, but she did not. Her mom informed her it was because she finished twelfth.

This motivated her to practice harder and dedicate herself to the sport. Kristi went on to win the 1992 Olympic figure skating championship as well as two world championships and the 2008 *Dancing with the Stars* competition.

Wisdom

Derive success from failure. When is a twelfth-place finish not a twelfth-place finish? When it motivates you to do better next time. If a poor finish causes you give up, maybe you weren't going to be a winner anyway.

The path to wisdom and remarkability is difficult and indirect. If Olympic gold medals were easy, more people would do it. Don't get me wrong: I'm not saying a poor finish is a good thing, nor that it will spur everyone to success.

But like bad starts, poor results, and mistaken identities, what really matters is what happens after these events occur.

3 | Inspiration

Inspiration exists, but it has to find you working.
—Pablo Picasso

Inspiration: the process of being mentally stimulated to do or feel something, especially to do something creative.

The Original Two Guys in a Garage

Hewlett-Packard was the inspiration for a generation of entrepreneurs in the 1970s and 1980s. This story had a huge impact on me and many other dreamers who believed "two guys in a garage" could start a big company.

The story begins in 1935 when Bill Hewlett and David Packard graduated from Stanford with electrical engineering degrees. To launch the company, they rented a one-car garage at 367 Addison Street in Palo Alto, California.

They flipped a coin to decide on the company's name—thus, the company could have been called Packard-Hewlett. The initial capital outlay was a grand total of $538, and first-year sales were $5,369.

The company's first product was an audio oscillator known as the HP 200A. An audio oscillator generates a pure tone or frequency that is used for music production. Walt Disney Studios was Hewlett-Packard's first customer, buying eight for the 1940 production of the movie *Fantasia*.

To understand the setting, I'll let Julie Packard, David Packard's daughter, describe the scene back then:

> Back then it was just apricot orchards and oak forest. There was hardly any urbanization at all, and so it was very rural and a lot quieter back then. Growing up, probably like most kids in the fifties, my dad worked all the time. No surprise.
>
> My dad bought this apricot orchard. We spent our summers in the orchard cutting the apricots to make dried apricots to sell. My dad loved vegetable gardening and growing stuff. He was this huge nature lover, but it had to be functional—hunting, fishing, growing things, cattle ranching.

> He loved driving tractors. He'd get out of the tractor and, like, adjust the orchard every spring and drive the tractor around, and then the summer apricots would be harvested, and we'd sell them to the canneries.

David Packard and Bill Hewlett were the fathers of Silicon Valley. Their company showed what was possible to people like college dropouts Steve Wozniak and Steve Jobs. And the rest is history.

Wisdom

Hewlett-Packard showed that a mega trend can start from simplicity, resourcefulness, and determination. Bill and Dave's journey from a garage to starting the tech revolution demonstrates how a simple idea can reverberate globally and inspire others to invent the future.

I'm not saying that if it wasn't for Hewlett-Packard we would still be using telegraphs and slide rulers, because someone would have invented the tech that surrounds us today. But they started the ball rolling and made it easier for all of us who followed.

So start small, boil a teapot ("oscillators"), not the ocean ("tech"), and keep at it.

The Book That Changed My Life

In 1987, my wife gave me *If You Want to Write* by Brenda Ueland, a writing professor at the University of Minnesota. At the time, I thought I wanted to write a book, but I wasn't sure that I was "a writer."

The book inspired me more than any other book I've ever read, and I've been recommending it for the past thirty years. Thousands of people read it as a result of my advice, and no one has given me negative feedback.

Inspiration 33

If You Want to Write encouraged me to think freely, creatively, and boldly. Even though I was not an "author" in anyone's mind, including my own, it enabled me to write my first book, *The Macintosh Way*. It helped me become a writer by reducing the constraints I placed on myself.

Here are three quotes from *If You Want to Write* that will whet your appetite for reading it:

> "Everyone is talented, original, and has something important to say."
>
> "Be careless, reckless! Be a lion, be a pirate, when you want to write."
>
> "Women should neglect their housework to write."

The book had a far-reaching impact on my writing career and my entire approach to life. The title is *If You Want to Write*, but you can substitute any creative endeavor and most vocations for the word "write."

For example, if you want to develop software, if you want to start a company, if you want to make movies, if you want to paint, if you want to surf, if you want to do almost anything . . .

Wisdom

I am living proof that a book can change a person's life. It catalyzed a lifelong goal for me: to write a book that helped as many people as possible.

Read *If You Want to Write*. Full stop. There is no greater recommendation than an author urging you to read a book that he did not write.

And give books that inspired you to others who can use the inspiration too. Plant those seeds that can become mighty oaks.

Jane Goodall, Secretary

Remarkable people often recount their childhood experiences in order to explain where they ended up. For example, here is Jane Goodall reminiscing about her youth in the 1930s:

> I used to roam on the cliffs with my dog, and that's where I watched the birds and the squirrels, read *Dr. Doolittle*, and I wished I could have a parrot to teach me animal language. And when I was eight, I pretended to all my friends that I could understand. I interpreted the dogs barking and the cats meowing and the birds singing.

Jane Goodall's family couldn't afford to send her to college, so she attended secretarial school to learn how to type, take shorthand, and do bookkeeping. Jane traveled to Nairobi in 1957 because of her fascination with animals and Africa.

She met Louis Leakey, the British anthropologist who documented the origin of human beings in East Africa. It just so happened that Leakey's secretary was leaving, so Jane could fill that position and remain in Africa.

In 1960, Leakey sent Jane to study chimpanzees living near a lake in Tanganyika. Jane's fascination with chimpanzees began when she was in her mid-twenties and lasted for sixty years. She proved that chimpanzees were not simply wild animals but were intelligent and highly social.

By 2023, Goodall had received honorary doctorates from more than seventy universities. She is a member of the National Academy of Sciences and the Royal Society of London. She was named one of *Time* magazine's 100 most influential people in the world in 2018, and in 2021 she received the Templeton Prize, given for achievements in scientific and spiritual curiosity.

Wisdom

Jane Goodall's narrative is a masterclass in seizing opportunities. As a child she roamed cliffs with her dog and fantasized about communicating with animals and later became a pioneer in primatology. Her life demonstrates that true calling often finds us when we indulge our early interests.

What's matters is not the path you start on. It's about seizing serendipitous good fortune like filling in as Louis Leakey's secretary and running with it. Just keep your eyes open, and never let go of your curiosity.

"I Have ALS. Why Don't I Complete Fifty Marathons?"

In 2014, Andrea Lytle Peet was diagnosed with ALS, a degenerative nerve disease that destroys cells in the brain and spinal cord. Most people succumb to ALS within two to five years as they lose their ability to eat, breathe, walk, and speak.

So far Andrea has survived for eleven years. Following her diagnosis, she had a brave idea: complete a marathon in all fifty states to defy the disease and to raise funds to find its cure. This is what Andrea Lytle Peet went through after learning of her ALS diagnosis:

> I remember just after my diagnosis I was sitting in the car crying. I was so depressed, and I looked up and I just realized that I can be depressed, or I can live my life now. Time will pass the same way either way.

She began her quest running on two legs but ended it in a recumbent trike. She achieved her goal in May 2022 in Prince of Wales Island, Alaska. Striving to complete fifty marathons after a diagnosis of a deadly nerve disease is the embodiment of embracing vulnerability and being inspiring.

Wisdom

To be blunt, shit is going to happen. You will face negativity, rejection, and even danger. People will tell you that what you want to do cannot be done, should not be done, and isn't necessary.

Andrea Lytle Peet's story is a profound example of resilience and the power of choice. After being diagnosed with ALS, she faced the grim statistics and decided to embrace bravery, defying expectations by completing marathons in all fifty states.

So "go on and be brave" (like the name of the movie about her) like Andrea. Her story teaches us that how we respond when life throws its toughest challenges at us defines our legacy.

From Prisoner to Painter

Halim Flowers had twenty-two years to prepare for his art career. In 1988, at the age of seventeen, he was convicted of aiding and abetting a felony murder. He was sentenced to two terms: forty years and twenty-to-life.

Halim grew up in Washington, DC, which was then known as the "murder capital" of the United States, with the highest homicide rate in the country. His father was a crack addict and few of his peers survived the drugs and crime.

In 2019, Halim was released after twenty-two years and two months of imprisonment because of the passage of a law that enabled convicts to be re-sentenced if they committed their crime before they were eighteen and had served at least fifteen years.

While in prison he became a peer counselor, an activist, and the author of eleven books. He enrolled in the Georgetown Prison and Justice Initiative to become a credit-earning student at Georgetown University. He also served as a mentor in the Young Men Emerging unit inside prison.

Inspiration 37

Halim has exhibited at the Philips Theological Seminary, Nicole Longnecker Gallery, MoMA PS1, and the National Arts Club in NYC. His art is for sale in the DTR Modern gallery in Georgetown, where he is the second black artist to be exhibited. The first was Jean Michel Basquiat—which is mighty fine company to be in.

He has sold more than $3 million of art through DTR Modern alone, and he's started a nonprofit called Artonomics, an organization that helps artists master the business of art by bridging creativity and commerce.

Wisdom

Halim Flowers exemplifies the concept of turning hardship into opportunity. What strikes me the most about Halim is his determination not to let external circumstances shape his identity or future.

Given his circumstances, society would have expected him to fall into oblivion if not death. Instead, he turned his circumstances—even one as difficult as prison—into a catalyst for change, demonstrating that extraordinary people frequently have origins in significant hardships.

Consider Halim's prison sentence as an unintended incubation period. He used those years to develop a rich inner life through reading, writing, and mentoring. His ability to transition from a life of crime to one of art and advocacy exemplifies the power of preparation and opportunity.

From Illegal to Inspiration

In 1976, Martha Niño's family relocated from Pueblo Viejo, Zacatecas, Mexico (population 300) to the United States. She was separated from her parents because she might make too much noise and smuggled into the United States by "coyotes" posing as her parents.

Her actual parents crossed the border illegally and separately. They hoped they would be reunited with their baby, but there was no guarantee. And many families who did the same thing were not reunited again.

Her family settled in California, working various jobs while living in a one-bedroom duplex with several other families. They hid for years from *la migra* and would duck and hide whenever neighbors shouted those frightening words.

Martha went to school and worked to support her family. A guidance counselor at her school assisted her in balancing work and school, allowing her to graduate on time.

Martha worked in warehouses and furniture manufacturing before moving on to temporary positions in tech companies such as Creative Labs and Handspring. She pursued a college degree after observing her colleagues make advances because of their education.

Martha eventually became a temporary contractor at graphics software company Adobe in 2003. She worked hard and earned a permanent position as a marketing manager at Adobe. By 2023, she authored a book titled *The Other Side: From a Shack to Silicon Valley* and became an activist for diversity and inclusion for the next generation of immigrants.

Wisdom

Martha's journey epitomizes the American Dream: Start as an illegal alien, stay out of trouble to avoid deportation, get an education, work hard, succeed, and then pay back.

To be fair, her story required the sacrifice and tenacity of her parents, assistance from mentors, her own efforts, a workable immigration law, and good fortune. But it shows what can be done.

Inspiration 39

Make Yourself Indispensable

Andrew Zimmern, TV personality and master of meals, menus, and meringue, shared his uplifting story with me. As a young man, he was addicted to drugs until he got his act together in his early thirties.

At that point, he was eager to do anything to develop his career, so he took on three unpaid internships at once. He received job offers from all three organizations, which is pretty damn inspiring.

A mentor of his offered him the advice that powered him to success, and I want to pass it along to you:

Make yourself indispensable.

Andrew told me how to achieve this lofty goal:

Show up: Indispensable people show up and do the work. Dispensable people don't. It's that simple. It makes no difference whether this takes place in real life or online.

Do the shit work nobody else wants to do: Doing whatever is necessary, no matter how unappealing, is a great way to show that you are valuable and to separate yourself from the pack.

Expand your skill set: The more skills that you have, the more you can accomplish. And the more you can accomplish, the more valuable you are.

Own a niche: As you broaden your skill set, find a niche that you can own. That is, something only you can do or you can do best.

Set high standards: Apply your best efforts to all that you do. Being merely adequate and "good enough" isn't good enough to be indispensable.

Make your boss look good: If your boss looks good, you look good too. If your boss does well, you do well. Your professional lives are intertwined. Making your boss look bad is not going to help you.

Andrew showed up early and consistently; did the shit work of cleaning sets; learned how to do makeup, sound, lighting, and guest booking; and mastered a niche like programming teleprompters—which made his boss look good.

Wisdom

Andrew Zimmern's journey from addiction to success illustrates a powerful truth: Making yourself indispensable opens doors. He dove into doing shit work, paid his dues, and broadened his skill set for the win. That's why Andrew Zimmern is Andrew Zimmern.

I hate to burst your bubble, but work–life balance is what you want to achieve over the course of your life. However, at any given point, you may be working more than balancing or balancing more than working. But, best case, work–life balance happens over the course of your life, not every day.

The Story of Canva

Canva's journey began in Melanie Perkins's mother's living room in Perth, Australia. At the University of Western Australia, Melanie recognized that design software was complex and expensive, frustrating students trying to design.

Seeing this pain as an opportunity, she and co-founder Cliff Obrecht launched Fusion Books. This company enabled students and teachers to create yearbooks easily and was a stepping stone to starting Canva in 2013.

Circa 2025, Canva has 225 million monthly active users, and it's valued at $40 billion. It has enabled millions of people to be

Inspiration 41

better communicators by empowering them to create their own graphics.

Melanie had to pitch the company to approximately 300 investors over three years to raise funding. The reasons for rejection were many, including the company's location in Australia, the dominance of Adobe as the *de facto* standard in graphics software, and probably that Melanie was a woman.

If she had given up on raising capital after the first 299 rejections, there might be no Canva today.

Wisdom

First, don't generalize a negative response. If one investor doesn't want to invest, don't conclude that your company is not fundable. If one company doesn't offer you a job, don't conclude you're unemployable.

Second, don't consider "no" a permanent decision. When you hear it, interpret the response as "not yet." Then take advantage of it to learn from the rejection and to keep trying. If you do so, the "no" may transform into a "yes."

The Lesson of My Missing Shrimp Tacos

In the summer of 2023, I purchased a substantial takeout order from Ranch Milk Mexican Grill in Watsonville, California. The chef forgot to include the four shrimp tacos I ordered. The next time I visited, I mentioned this, and the counter clerk instantly insisted on giving me four shrimp tacos based solely on my word.

When I told this story to some friends, they both told me that her decision was a common kind of reaction and therefore no big deal. I disagreed, so I checked with two experts: Andrew Zimmern (television host) and Roy Yamaguchi (creator of Roy's Restaurants).

> *Andrew Zimmern:* It's overdelivering in many ways, but more owners should empower their frontline workers to handle stuff exactly this way. I bet you will go back again and again to this place. That's real hospitality and more people should operate that way but few do.

> *Roy Yamaguchi:* My initial reaction would be awesome, what great customer service. When an employee takes action and finds solutions to a problem, this is priceless. Getting an okay sometimes from a manager doesn't produce the same feeling when it's done in an instant.

Don't get me wrong: it's wonderful when you or your organization overdelivers in big ways such as an electric car that goes further than its official rating, but the little things are meaningful too.

Wisdom

The lesson here is to trust people and assume they are good until proven bad. This is what happened in my case of the missing tacos. The counter clerk trusted that I wasn't trying to scam her out of four tacos.

Financially, the gain in positive karma, loyalty, and word-of-mouth reputation outweighs the potential loss from being scammed out of four tacos. The fear that "everyone says they didn't get the complete order and wants a replacement" will not happen.

Pick Up the Turtle

Sarah Frey is a produce and beverage mogul. Her company has 35,000 points of distribution, and her products account for 200 million servings in the United States per year, circa 2025.

When she was approximately nine years old, she and her father were driving a pickup truck in rural Illinois. They happened upon

Inspiration

a garbage-can-sized snapping turtle weighing thirty-five or forty pounds. Her father told her to grab it and throw it in the back of the truck so they could eat it.

She eventually got the courage to do this. They're not called snapping turtles for nothing, and they are especially aggressive on land. In our interview on *Remarkable People*, she credits this formative experience with helping her overcome later challenges, such as making sales calls on Walmart.

I've been to the Walmart headquarters in Bentonville, Arkansas, to sell it stuff. There are dozens of numbered rooms. You get called to a room, and the rigor begins. You have no power in the belly of this beast. It is truly an intimidating process.

Wisdom

The moral of Sarah Frey's story is that facing your fears head-on can fuel future success. By tackling the challenge of dealing with that snapping turtle, she learned to conquer her fears, paving the way for bold business moves like selling to Walmart.

I'm not saying you should purposely risk life and limb, but if you never face any fear, you will not be prepared for the inevitable challenges in life.

Fail Like Apple

Apple, one of the most valuable companies of all time, failed with the Apple III, Lisa, Newton, Pippin, and iPod Hi-Fi. You may never have heard of these Apple products, and I won't even take up space explaining what they were.

Failing in a careless, unconcerned, or offhand manner is not okay. Failure is a waste of money, time, effort, and human potential. It can harm the careers of employees, and in extreme cases it can endanger the lives of customers (here's looking at you, Theranos) and vendors.

Failures provide valuable information that improves future efforts. They are not simply a waste of time and resources. And you could not have obtained this information in any other way than risking failure. Here are three examples from the field of entertainment:

Walt Disney was fired from one of his first animation jobs because the editor felt he lacked imagination.

Oprah Winfrey was fired from her first job in television as a news anchor in Baltimore.

Steven Spielberg was rejected by the USC film school multiple times.

The point is that failure is less destructive and sometimes even constructive if it can be transformed into something that ultimately strengthens you. The path to remarkableness is not paved.

Wisdom

After seventy years, I have come to the realization that hiding your failures is a waste of time. To begin with, few people will probably notice when you flop, fizzle, or misfire. And those who do notice won't care or remember it.

Transforming failure into a stepping stone rather than a stumbling block is the hallmark of all remarkable journeys. Real progress is often spurred by the lessons that failure brings, and every misstep is simply another wave setting you up for the next big ride.

Whether you're falling off a surfboard or driving innovation at a company like Apple, the goal is to learn and adapt—turning flops into fuel for future success.

4 | Realization

The harder the struggle, the more glorious the triumph.
—Swami Sivananda

Realization: an act of becoming fully aware of something as a fact.

Look Beyond Money

In 2010, I asked a longtime Apple employee why he remained at the company. By that time, it was difficult to make much money on Apple stock (boy, was I wrong about that!). Plus, he worked in a part of Apple that had frequent interactions directly with Steve Jobs—that is, Steve drilled them constantly.

The employee's answer stunned me: "I stay at Apple because it enables me to do the best work of my career. Every company has bullshit, but at least at Apple, I know that the person at the top knows when I do good work."

So true. Unlike Jobs, the top management of most tech companies cannot judge whether products are good. They throw around words like "revolutionary," "innovative," and "disruptive," but they really don't know good stuff when they see it, and they certainly have difficulty inspiring good stuff.

That is one reason why there are so many mediocre and ugly products—and why Jobs and Apple crushed the competition for several decades.

Wisdom

Don't assume that the only motivational tools for employee recruitment and retention are money and fringe benefits. There are always organizations that can pay more or provide better perks.

The opportunity to learn new skills, operate independently, contribute to a higher purpose, and work for people who have the smarts to know when you've done good work is rare and valuable.

If you're an employee, look beyond salary and perks. Does the job enable you to master new skills while working autonomously towards a meaningful goal?

If you're a boss, are you offering employees a way to master new skills while working autonomously towards a meaningful goal?

You Can Teach an Old Dog New Tricks

I cannot say that I am a remarkable hockey player or surfer. I took up these sports at the ages of forty-four and sixty, respectively. This means that I started thirty-four and fifty years too late, respectively.

My sons wanted to play hockey after we attended a San Jose Sharks game, so I started playing hockey even though I was old and from Hawaii. The closest thing to pond hockey where I grew up is shave ice.

In 2015, I started surfing because of my daughter. She was fourteen, and I was sixty. Despite growing up in Hawaii, I didn't have enough of a growth mindset to try something outside of organized team sports.

I embraced these new sports because Brenda Ueland and Carol Dweck profoundly impacted my mindset. Ueland, who I mentioned earlier, was a teacher of writing at the University of Minnesota and author the book *If You Want to Write*.

In 2006, Carol Dweck, a professor of psychology at Stanford University, released her book *Mindset: The New Psychology of Success*.

Her insights were like Ueland's but on steroids. Her book convinced me that growth can happen along any path that you let it. At the time, I was fat, dumb, and happy concentrating on what worked for me in the past. I certainly wasn't taking up any new sports.

Dweck didn't just dent my universe, she expanded it. I had written a few books, but I was afraid of failure and embarrassment in other fields. Here is Carol's explanation of the fixed and growth mindsets:

> The fixed mindset is the belief that your qualities are carved in stone. The growth mindset is the belief that your qualities can be cultivated through effort.

Realization 49

People with a fixed mindset make statements such as "I'm too old to learn a new skill." Or "I'm good at programming, but I could never learn marketing." By contrast, people with a growth mindset are willing, even eager, to explore and experiment.

Undoubtedly, the growth mindset is necessary to be remarkable. You hold the power to change and elevate yourself, so you must affirm this about yourself and others. Full stop. Not negotiable.

Wisdom

Hockey and surfing were difficult at my advanced age but embracing these sports provided some of the most satisfying moments of my life. My moderate success showed me the benefits of a growth mindset and, more importantly, set my expectations to be able to learn new skills in general.

My hockey and surfing sagas taught me at least four life lessons:

First, don't let anyone tell you that it's too late to try new endeavors. This applies to the naysayer and critic inside of you—self-doubt is a bitch. According to generally accepted wisdom, I started hockey thirty-five years and surfing fifty years too late.

Second, be willing to grit it out. My path to hockey and surfing competency were not fast, smooth, or easy. They were, in fact, the same as my path for speaking, writing, and evangelizing: grit, repetition, and hard work, not "natural talent."

Third, get the right equipment. There's a theory that if you're good enough, the equipment doesn't matter—along the lines of "It's the photographer, not the camera." This is fine if you're young, poor, and athletic. But if you're old, rich, and klutzy, you should use every means to succeed.

50 *Wiser Guy*

Fourth, find a coach or two. There's no way I would have achieved my prone surfing competency without coaches. In other words, work hard but also work smart by finding people who can help you. When you start at sixty, you don't have time to figure things out by yourself.

The Knight Who Shined My Shoes

In 2008, Richard Branson and I spoke at a conference in Moscow, Russia. This was the first time that we met. We were in the speaker prep room, and he asked me if I flew on Virgin—which is what you would expect him to ask.

I explained that I was a Global Services–level United Airlines customer—which meant free, automatic upgrades, and other VIP services. No one except United employees knows what it takes to achieve this exclusive status. Reaching it is not as simple as accumulating lots of miles.

I explained to Branson that I didn't want to jeopardize my Global Services status by flying on other airlines. Then he dropped to his knees and started polishing my shoes with his coat. That was the moment I decided to start flying on Virgin America. (I never saw Steve Jobs get on his knees to get a customer.)

Wisdom

Be humble—it will help you succeed. If a billionaire and knight who owns an island and kitesurfs with Barack Obama can get on his knees and shine someone's shoes, you can too. Perhaps his willingness to do this is *why* he became a billionaire and knight.

Skeptics would argue that Richard may only do this for people who are rich, famous, or powerful. But my sense of him is that he would have done this for anyone—he's that kind of person.

Realization 51

You Can't Go Wrong Starting in Sales

When I dropped out of law school, I wasn't done with formal education. I loved the whole concept of running a business and making money, so I entered the MBA program at UCLA.

There were only four days of classes per week because Friday was a day to gain real-world experience—or goof off. I got a part-time job counting diamonds and helping in the shipping and receiving department at a jewelry manufacturer called Nova Stylings. With a four-day week, I had plenty of time for a part-time job, and I needed spending money.

As a result, my life took an unpredictable turn, since "jeweler" was not one of the preferred career paths for Asian Americans. When I graduated from UCLA, I didn't interview with investment banks and consulting firms like my classmates did, because Nova Stylings made me an offer of money and responsibility that I couldn't refuse.

Working for Nova was one of the best decisions I ever made, because the CEO of the company, Marty Gruber, taught me one of the most valuable skills I ever learned: how to sell.

Jewelry is made of commodities—expensive commodities, but commodities nonetheless, and the jewelry business is also hand-to-hand combat. It is not the black magic of modern times involving search-engine optimization, A/B testing, big data, and email lists.

In the jewelry business, you haven't been a salesperson until a buyer for a jewelry store sticks your product on a scale, figures out how much gold is in it, and offers to pay you 10 percent over scrap value in 120 days. In six years in the jewelry business, I never heard the words "partnership" or "strategic" once.

On the other hand, I heard the phrase, "I can get the same designs for 50 percent cheaper" every day. In other words, the jewelry business was tougher than the tech business.

Wisdom

As I look back on my career, my six-year stint in a low-tech, family-owned company was the foundation of my future success as a tech evangelist because it taught me these lessons about sales:

First, pay the price. Much of sales is dealing with patience and enduring rejection. I might wait many hours for a chance to pitch our goods and then come away with no order. You learn to keep trying until you break through.

Second, earn people's trust. This means that you do what you say, and you say what you do. You don't take shortcuts, and you live up to your promises. And it's very hard to earn trust, but very easy to lose it.

Third, be likable. Sounds like a duhism, but at some level there are many adequate substitutes for almost everything. In these cases, the people will prefer to do business with people they like.

If you don't get an internship at Google, Facebook, or Apple, it's not the end of the world. In fact, you may develop a stronger foundation by *not* working in La La Land with volleyball courts and free food trying to figure out if the blue or the red border yields more click-throughs.

Fake It Until You Litigate It

During my first tour of duty at Apple, I had the privilege of working with Jack Brown of the law firm Brown and Bain. He and his firm represented Apple in the intellectual property lawsuits against Digital Research and Microsoft in the 1980s.

Apple sued Digital Research because it had created an operating system called GEM (graphical environment manager) that, at least according to us, ripped off the Macintosh graphical user interface. At the beginning of the lawsuit, Jack Brown, his team, and several of us from Apple went to Digital Research's office in Monterey to confront the company.

Realization

I drove down with Brown. For much of the trip, he told me how weak our case was because Xerox's Palo Alto Research Center had created a similar user interface before Apple. Also, according to Brown, "A window is a window, and a trash can is a trash can, you can't own such simple concepts." I got out of the car thinking that our lawsuit was doomed.

Then the meeting began, and he started with a ten-minute sermon about the immoral, heinous, and unconscionable crime that Digital Research had committed. I'm paraphrasing, but he went on the attack: "In my entire career I've never seen a more blatant transgression of intellectual property," and "I don't know why we're meeting. We should go straight to court."

These accusations flew through the air like tracer bullets from an A-10 Warthog. Less than an hour before he had told me we had no chance of winning. Now I was hearing that intellectual property law as well as the universe's moral compass were on our side. It was motherhood, apple pie, and the Macintosh user interface.

Wisdom

First, fortune favors the bold. This means that you make a bold claim, a large monetary amount if your selling, or small monetary amount out there if you're buying.

When Brown postulated that copying the Macintosh user interface was a heinous crime, it would have been difficult for Digital Research to counter that it was a minor mistake or transgression of copying the trash can icon.

Second, speak first and set the agenda. If Digital Research had spoken first, then it could have tried to claim that what it did was a minor mistake or transgression. Then it would take a master litigator/negotiator to continue to insist it was a heinous crime—which Brown was, so it wouldn't have worked.

54 Wiser Guy

Third, understand when you're being played. Assume that your adversary is trying to set the agenda and then don't play the game by those rules. Stake your own claim as if you didn't hear anything.

As the saying goes, "Fake it until you litigate it." That day Jack Brown made me a better negotiator for the rest of my life.

Look for Commonality

I once spoke to a Macintosh user group in Mobile, Alabama, and a white guy said to me, "You know Guy-ya, I was born too late for slavery and too early for robots."

I laughed when he said this, but I was thinking: "I may not be Black, but I'm not exactly white. Your people put my people in internment camps in World War II." If we didn't share a love of Macintosh, we might not have had a friendly encounter.

Making a difference and becoming remarkable necessitates building relationships and persuading people. You have a choice: You can focus on what divides you, or you can focus on what interests you share to foster a connection.

Wisdom

Find something to agree on. While Apple was trying to get the market to use Macintosh for word processing, spreadsheets, and databases, it finally found agreement with desktop publishing.

Points of commonality can also overcome unfamiliarity, differences, and even conflict between people. My user group friend saw me as part of the Macintosh tribe, not as a non-white guy who would find his reference to slavery offensive.

Thus, the lesson is to force yourself to interact with people— even your enemies—because more exposure increases the probability of finding commonality, developing empathy, and building a relationship.

God's gift for finding something in common with people is LinkedIn. There you can learn about their educational background, work experience, and social connections to you. It's the best tool ever for finding something on which to agree.

If you ever encounter me, feel free to ask me about BBQ, surfing, podcasting, and Macintosh. We will almost certainly end the conversation as friends. But please do not tell me that you enjoyed reading *Rich Dad, Poor Dad* or that you love my motorcycles.

Face It Until You Make It

Few activities are riskier than big-wave surfing. Any surfing is dangerous but imagine riding down the outside of a 100-foot-tall building moving at forty miles per hour. When such a wave crashes on you, this is what it feels like:

> Imagine you're in a washing machine on spin cycle and then for lack of a better person, King Kong grabs the washing machine and starts shaking it in all directions.

This description is from Garrett McNamara. He should know because he's the big-wave surfer who made the world aware of the waves at Nazaré, Portugal. Depending on who you believe, he may have surfed the largest wave in history. The HBO series *100 Foot Wave* is based on his adventures around the world.

If there's a person in the world to ask how to push past fear and vulnerability, Garrett is it. This is how he explained the process to me:

> When I was sixteen, I wouldn't go out over ten feet. I was terrified. I got pounded on a ten-foot wave, and I vowed never to surf a wave over ten feet.

> And then my buddies forced me to go out. They gave me the right board, gave me the right advice, and I caught every wave I wanted, and that was it.
>
> The fire was lit. I lived for big waves. I loved big waves from that day forward. It was ten feet and fifteen feet, then twenty feet, then twenty-five.
>
> I got pounded on a solid fifty-foot face . . . the worst you could ever get pounded and came up laughing. So then I was like, "I can handle anything."

There isn't "faking it until you make it" in big-wave surfing. Death and dismemberment are the risks—not simply bruised feelings or crushed egos. Garrett is saying that you must confront your fears, and eventually they can turn into excitement.

Wisdom

In the world of big-wave surfing, fear is your fiercest competitor, but once you confront it, the thrill outweighs the terror. Garrett McNamara shows us that battling our deepest fears head-on can transform vulnerability into success and accomplishment.

His journey from dread to dominance proves that real growth requires strapping in and riding those waves of adversity with a grin. That said, I won't surf in waves larger than five feet. Just saying.

You Never Know

C. P. Ellis was born in 1927 in Durham, North Carolina. He faced a life of limited education and extreme poverty. Seeking to fulfill a need for belonging and for someone to blame for his hardship, he joined the Ku Klux Klan.

Realization 57

He rose to the position of "exalted cyclops" of the Ku Klux Klan. Then in 1971 he was appointed to co-lead a community group that was facing the challenge of desegregating Durham's schools. The other leader was a Black activist named Ann Atwater.

To put it mildly, their relationship was contentious. For one thing, between 1865 and 1941, approximately 150 Black people were lynched in North Carolina. But by working together, the two developed a close relationship. Ellis renounced his membership in the Klan and tore up his membership card at a Klan meeting.

Atwater even delivered the eulogy at Ellis's funeral in 2005. This is a powerful example of the realization that relationships can change as people get to know each other.

Wisdom

C. P. Ellis's journey shows that our worst divides can be bridged when we focus on shared goals—you never know, even with those we'd least expect. His transformation from Klan leader to civil rights ally illustrates the profound power of connection and understanding.

This story reminds us that building relationships can dismantle long-held prejudices, proving that change starts with courage and willingness to embrace empathy.

So Much for Selling Pez Dispensers

Pierre Omidyar, the founder of eBay, tells this story about the origin of the company: His girlfriend at the time (now wife) collected Pez dispensers, and she needed a way to sell them online. Since there wasn't a way, he started eBay.

However, Omidyar told me that this was a total bullshit story. His intention was to create a "perfect market" for the efficient pricing of goods—where the demand and supply curves intersect.

58 Wiser Guy

This explanation, however, did not intrigue the press, so a PR person invented the Pez story.

People and companies love to use adjectives to describe what they do. I wish I had a dollar for every time I heard a pitch for a "revolutionary, patent-pending, curve-jumping, innovative, scalable, enterprise-class product created by rockstar programmers."

Because everyone goes on adjective binges, these pitches are ineffective. Adjectives would work if everyone else described their product as "slow, buggy, hard-to-use, and pieces of crap," but that's not what happens. Everyone claims to have a great product. Hence, the effectiveness of stories in an adjective-infested world.

Wisdom

A memorable story often becomes the cornerstone of how people perceive your brand or product, far beyond technical jargon. This is why when Pierre Omidyar's myth about eBay's origin involving Pez dispensers took off, it captivated people's imaginations far better than his original, more technical vision.

Stories simplify the complex, transforming dry facts into a narrative that's engaging and easy to remember. While everyone in the industry rushes to declare their product as "innovative" or "cutting-edge," a compelling story cuts through the noise.

There's Always a Way

One of my sons flunked his driving test twice. In California, if you fail a third time, you must start the entire license application process over. This would mean getting another permit after a cooling-off period, retaking the written test, and then taking the driving test again.

Realization 59

To ensure that he didn't flunk a third time, we drove to the local Department of Motor Vehicles and followed several of its examiners as they took applicants on the road for driving tests. Then we drove each route several times for practice.

My son got a perfect score on the third try, and I earned major dad credibility. Maybe I even taught him a life lesson.

Wisdom

Figure out a way to prepare for every test, interview, or challenge. There's always a method. However, three factors can get in your way.

First, arrogance: "I don't need to prepare. I'll rise to the occasion." Second, laziness: "I'm too busy to prepare." Third, stupidity: "I'm probably going to fail, so I won't prepare. Then when I fail, I'll prove myself right."

People who prepare the most are the "luckiest," and preparation trumps "natural ability" almost every time. If you prepare and have natural ability, you're unbeatable.

The Truth Helps You Keep Your Job

One day sometime in 1984, Jobs appeared in my cubicle with a man that I didn't know. He didn't introduce him—Jobs wasn't long on social niceties. Instead, he asked, "What do you think of a company called Knoware?"

I told Jobs that the company's products were mediocre, boring, and simplistic and that the company was not strategic for us. After all, they didn't take advantage of the Macintosh graphical user interface and other advanced features.

After my diatribe, Jobs said to me, "I want you to meet the CEO of Knoware, Archie McGill." I shook his hand, and Steve said to him, "See? That's what I told you."

Thank you, Steve.

60 Wiser Guy

In the Macintosh Division, you had to prove yourself every day. Steve demanded excellence and kept you at the top of your game. It wasn't easy to work for him; it was sometimes unpleasant and always scary, but it drove many of us to do the finest work of our careers.

If I had said nice things about the crappy Knoware products, Steve would have, at a minimum, decided that I was clueless, and that would have limited my career at Apple. At worst, he would have said that I was shit and fired me later that day, if not on the spot.

Wisdom

Honesty is a test of your competence and character. You need intelligence to recognize what is true, and you need strength to speak it. The wiser the person, the more they yearn for the truth. Telling people that their product is good just to be kind doesn't help them improve it—much less fool people like Steve.

Honesty is not only better, it's also easier. There's only one truth, so being consistent is simple if you're honest. If you are not honest, you have to concoct a lie and then keep track of what you said.

Send the Right Signals

The best-laid incentive plans can go awry. It's from an article called "The Great Hanoi Rat Hunt: A Conversation with Michael G. Vann." Vietnamese officials in Hanoi paid a bounty for rat tails because of an infestation of the pests from China.

Citizens turned in hundreds of thousands of tails for bounties, but the program was *curtailed* when officials discovered people were breeding rats, cutting off their tails, and then releasing them to foster more breeding. People even collected rats from outside Hanoi.

Realization 61

Can you fault them? The incentive was to turn in as many rats as you could. Better ways include an educational program about the diseases rats transmit, free resources such as poison and traps, and public certification of rat-free buildings.

Bob Cialdini, godfather of influence, might advocate social pressure: "Our neighbor's house has a sign that it is rat-free. We need to keep up with them and not endanger our neighborhood too."

Wisdom

The message is to ensure that your incentives and objectives are aligned. Generally, people will do what you reward them for doing, not necessarily what you discuss conceptually.

For example, if you pay annual bonuses but try to emphasize the long-term well-being of an organization, guess what will happen when people can choose between locking in a good year and the "long run."

Another example: Imagine the difference in results when you pay people per hour versus completed piece. It gets complicated though because paying people per piece may make them rush and lower quality. But paying them per hour may make them work slower, not better.

What Makes People Happy

The Harvard Study of Adult Development is a long-term research project that started in 1938 and is the longest of its kind. It has tracked the lives of hundreds of individuals over an extended period to unlock the secrets of happiness and well-being.

It started with approximately 700 men who were either sophomores at Harvard or from Boston's poorest neighborhoods. Over time, 1,300 of their descendants were added to the study, which has now gone on for over eight decades.

62   Wiser Guy

Robert Waldinger, the fourth leader of the study, told me in our interview that happiness is deeply tied to **strong, meaningful connections** with others.

The key isn't the quantity of friends or acquaintances, much less money and toys, but the depth and authenticity of those relationships, or quality.

So investing time and energy into fostering these bonds can profoundly impact your overall happiness and well-being.

Wisdom

Happiness isn't in the number of friends but in the strength and authenticity of connections. It's in nurturing ties that are deep and meaningful. The study has been an eight-decade revelation that life satisfaction is deeply tied to investing in real relationships.

The smart move is to channel energy into the relationships that matter. Here's where you can create true impact by fostering empathy and compassion. That effort becomes your legacy and transformation in real-time, yielding both immediate and enduring happiness. Relationships don't just fill the gaps—they build bridges.

Remember, quality, not quantity.

5 | Exhortation

Small deeds done are better than great deeds planned.
—Peter Marshall

Exhortation: an address or communication emphatically urging someone to do something.

Put Skills First

In the quest to hire better than yourself, the most important quality is the skills people bring to a job. There are multiple paths to achieve these skills, including formal education, work experience, and training. However, people seem always to focus on formal education the most.

Ginni Rometty, the first female CEO of IBM, embraced this concept because she saw that many positions at IBM required a college degree even though the actual work didn't.

This is her epiphany about hiring non-degreed people:

> We do a lot of data gathering over the years and we find that after about a year, they show the same performance as our college grads. They're taking more courses because they're thirsty. They want to keep learning. More loyal, more retentive.
>
> Eventually it takes me down a decade of work where we would re-look at every job credential, and we find that 50 percent of our jobs did not need to start with a college degree.

Remember, this is coming from the former CEO of a company with 350,000 employees, universal brand awareness, and unlimited resources! If she can look beyond degrees, you can too.

Using a personal example, when I hired Madisun, she had no formal background in podcasting, writing, or administrative work. Her academic background was holistic medicine. But she sure had the drive, work ethic, and brains to master all three.

And you'll soon learn what little qualifications I had to be Apple's software evangelist.

Wisdom

Ginni's and Madisun's stories illustrate how skills trump degrees. When you go beyond traditional credentials, you discover untapped talent eager to learn, adapt, and grow. Ginni Rometty's insight at IBM is a testament to looking past the paper to see practical potential.

Madisun's knack for learning and determination was more valuable than any degree. This approach spices up your team with loyalty and innovation, transforming your workplace into a well-oiled machine. Remember, credentials might open doors, but skills produce success.

Ask What's Missing

Many authors and experts delight in telling the story of Steve Jobs (Reed College), Bill Gates (Harvard University), and Mark Zuckerberg (Harvard University) dropping out of college but still succeeding.

This is the time-honored tradition of studying successful people or companies and then labeling what they share as the cause of their success. In this case, the implications are that dropouts make great entrepreneurs, and a college education isn't necessary to succeed.

A study by Chris Chabris, a research psychologist at Union College, found that in 2015 all the CEOs of the 253 "unicorns" (private companies with a valuation of at least $1 billion) had college degrees. And this is a snapshot of only 2015, whereas the cherry-picked examples of Jobs, Gates, and Zuckerberg span decades.

If you only consider the handful of highly successful entrepreneurs without college degrees, what's missing are the facts that there are far more successful entrepreneurs who have

Exhortation   67

college degrees as well as many unsuccessful entrepreneurs without college degrees.

Maybe it is a good idea to get a college degree after all . . .

Wisdom

The wisdom here is the necessity to develop the power of "discernment." This is the ability to wisely judge and distinguish between what is true and false, good and bad, important and unimportant, complete and incomplete.

Discernment will help you decide when to listen, when to ignore, and when to challenge. Four successful entrepreneurs without college degrees? Then ask how many people without college degrees could not advance. And how many people with college degrees could.

Just Say Yes

Derek Sivers, a musician, circus ringleader, entrepreneur, programmer, author, and TED speaker, told me this story about the start of his career:

> I was seventeen years old, and my friend had an agent. His agent called him, and said, "Hey, there's a pig show that pays $75 for you to go play some strolling music. Will you do it?"
>
> . . . I didn't care that I was going to make a whopping $20 because this was my first paying gig ever. I was given really no instruction. Just get on this bus, go to this place.
>
> . . . I just walked around this pig show with a guitar on my neck just playing guitar. I got back on the bus to Boston, and then the agent called me, and said, "This is Greg Merrill. I heard you did a really good job at the pig show. . . . I want

you to play at the art gallery opening. If you do well at the art opening, then you're in the circus."

That's how I got my job in the circus, which ended up being over 1,000 shows. Eventually I started making $300 per show and performed 1,000 shows around the northeast US. It was an amazing stage experience . . .

All of these things, such a massive experience, because I said yes to the $75 pig-show gig . . . I just said yes to everything, which is a wonderful strategy early in your career.

Wisdom

The story of Derek Sivers teaches us that saying yes to small, seemingly insignificant opportunities can unlock a world of possibilities. By embracing unexpected gigs, Derek discovered adventures that molded his career and creativity. It's a testament that greatness often starts in the humblest settings, a reminder to seize each chance—even those worth just $75.

My advice, even to my own kids, is to just say yes, and then figure it out. Because of YouTube and LLMs, everything you need to learn is probably explained out there.

Remove Friction

During the 2017 SXSW conference in Austin, Texas, I made a video with the chair of Mercedes-Benz, Dieter Zetsche. The producer of the video wanted me in a plain T-shirt, so I had to scramble to find one at the last minute, since every T-shirt I own has some company's logo on it.

The closest clothing store to my hotel was a Bonobos outlet on 2nd Street, so I headed there with only thirty minutes before the recording was due to start. After walking five blocks in the heat of a sunny Austin day, I found the store and selected two

Exhortation

69

T-shirts. I waited several minutes for the clerk and finally got some attention.

First, he asked me for my email address. This was odd for a retail store, but I gave him the benefit of the doubt because I appreciate lead generation. But then he asked me for my physical address. I asked him why, and he said, "We have to ship the shirts to you. You cannot get them here."

I was amazed. I asked him why this was the policy, and he said that if customers took delivery in the store, there wouldn't be samples to show others. I was dumbfounded. I gave him the T-shirts back and walked out. A block away, I found a store that did me the honor of selling and handing me a T-shirt.

Wisdom

First, take a sale when you can. The moment people walk out of your store or navigate from your website, you've lost them. One of the few advantages a brick-and-mortar store may retain over Amazon (though Amazon is experimenting with brick-and-mortar stores, so this advantage may not last long either) is instant gratification, and Bonobos threw it away.

Also, never ask people to do something you wouldn't do. I find it hard to believe that Bonobos execs and their families would prefer to go clothes shopping and come home with a stack of email confirmations for orders.

Experience as Currency

Consider working for free. Ade Harnusa Azril, an electrical engineering undergraduate student at Institut Teknolgi Bandung in Indonesia, came up with the concept for the cover of one of my books, *Enchantment*. I found him by running an online design contest.

Here's how the contest worked. I used my social media accounts to announce that I was looking for a cover design. I provided the basic specifications for the cover, such as the title and subtitle, and then let anyone submit ideas. To my delight, 250 people submitted 760 designs.

I selected Azril's design and paid him $1,000. The story gets interesting because of the vitriol the contest aroused. People complained that a design contest exploited designers, and they stated they would boycott the book and tell everyone they knew not to read it.

Their argument was that I was able to pick from the work of 250 people but paid only one. Thus, I exploited everyone who entered the contest but did not win. Furthermore, I set a precedent that conducting a contest was acceptable, which would lead to more contests taking place and the exploitation of even more designers.

According to "general" industry practices, a client is supposed to meet with a handful of designers, explain the project, request proposals (but not designs), and then make a choice. Only one designer works on the project, and they are paid for that work.

I wanted to give anyone in the world a chance to design my cover—not only people who were already bona fide "designers" and within my immediate reach. And I didn't want to limit my choices to one designer's concepts. However, these two goals crossed the boundaries of many designers.

The contest enabled me to get a cover that delighted me, and I helped Azril's career as well as put some money in his pocket. I doubt that the boycott, real or threatened, had an impact on the sale of the book. I would do it again in a second.

Wisdom

First, do what it takes and pay the price of success. Writers enter writing contests. Musicians play on street corners. Programmers participate in hackathons. Contestants on *America's Got Talent*

Exhortation 71

don't get paid. I have given dozens of free speeches, and they led to paid ones. The sheer quantity of speeches that I've delivered helped me improve, too.

Second, reach out and grab opportunities and wrestle them to the ground. Do it for no pay or low pay. Exploitation can be a state of mind, just like being a victim, not pegged to compensation. TEDx, for example, doesn't pay speakers, but you should jump at the chance to speak at a TEDx event for the validation and exposure.

What People Regret

Daniel Pink is an author, speaker, and host of the World Regret Project. The latter is a website where 19,000 people from 105 countries have revealed their regrets in life. His analysis of the results led to a book called *The Power of Regrets*.

We all have regrets—even remarkable people—so we can learn from Daniel's findings to adjust our priorities and learn from the regrets of others. In his own words, the top four types of regrets are:

Foundation regrets. People around the world regret not exercising enough, not taking care of their bodies, not studying hard enough in school, not saving money. This is when you didn't do the work, so you didn't get the reward.

Boldness regrets. Overwhelmingly, my research and other research reveals that people regret inactions way more than actions. They regret what they didn't do way more than what they did do. People regret not starting a business and staying in a lackluster job. I got huge numbers of people around the world regret not asking someone else on a date.

Connection regrets. These type of regrets make up the biggest category: regrets where there was a relationship, or there should have been a relationship, and somehow it

72   Wiser Guy

drifted apart. Among the things I discovered in looking at these is that the way our relationships come apart typically, is not dramatic. That is, we think that relationships come apart by some kind of blowout fight, and that's rarely the case. A lot of times, they just drift, and drift.

Moral regrets. I have found hundreds of people who regret bullying kids at school when they were younger. A woman I interviewed broke into tears recounting the story of bullying a kid when she was eight years old, and she's in her fifties.

What surprised me about his research is the boldness regret. I thought people would regret taking too many chances and regretting the failures. Instead, the opposite is true. This is good to know before it's too late.

Wisdom

Daniel Pink's World Regret Project uncovers a powerful insight: Life's real regrets stem from timidity and missed connections. It's not the leaps that haunt us but the chances we let slip by, and those relationships we let drift away. So if you want a remarkable life, leap boldly and nurture your bonds, because courage and connection make the journey worthwhile.

Relish the Shit Sandwich

I learned the real-world test to determine whether you have found your *ikigai*, or reason to get up every morning from Mark Manson, author of *The Subtle Art of Not Giving a F*ck: A Counterintuitive Approach to Living a Good Life*. He told me that you'll know you found your calling when you enjoy the shit sandwiches that it requires.

That is, you love to do what most people consider shit work. Writing involves the shit sandwich of rewriting and revising text

Exhortation

over and over and over. I spend hundreds of hours doing this for each book.

Here's the Gospel of Shit Sandwich from Mark. Come to find out, we share a love of the same shit sandwich!

> I kind of get a sick pleasure out of rewriting the same paragraph seven times. Most people don't though, but that's why I'm a writer and they're not. There are other people who really, really, really enjoy spreadsheets. And that's why they're an accountant or a data analyst or whatever.
>
> So instead of thinking about the benefits you want, think about the sacrifices that you enjoy . . . that most people don't 'cause that's where your competitive advantage is.

I hope that one day you will ask yourself, "Why do I enjoy this so much?" Or someone asks you with admiration, "Why do you do that crap?" That is the day that your *ikigai* has manifested, and I mean this in the most complimentary way: Your passion has turned to shit.

Wisdom

The lesson here is that true passion and purpose come from loving what others might see as a tedious ordeal. It's in those grit-filled moments that you find your true calling, your *ikigai*, because they don't feel like chores to you. Embrace the grind enthusiastically, and your efforts will naturally shine.

Simple Questions Yield Big Answers

In December 2015, I came across an example of an accidental innovation. There's a restaurant in Waipahu, Hawaii, called Honolulu Kitchen. Its specialty is fried manapua, which you may know by the more commonly used terms "pork buns" or "char siu bao." Trust me when I tell you that it's worth driving to Waipahu to try this restaurant.

The chef's wife told me that the idea for fried manapua happened by accident when her husband dropped one into a pot of hot oil. Rather than throwing away the manapua, he let it cook to see how it would taste. And the rest is Hawaiian culinary history.

Many people believe that entrepreneurs plan the evolution of their company on a linear and direct path. For example, they think that Bill Gates planned that Microsoft would sell operating systems, application software, game consoles, and enterprise software, and that Steve Jobs and Steve Wozniak planned to sell computers, tablets, phones, digital music, and apps.

The truth is probably that Bill Gates wanted to get IBM's business for the IBM PC, and he wasn't looking beyond that. And Steve and Woz wanted to sell some Apple Is to the Homebrew Computer Club. The long-term plan was "until we run out of money and have to get a real job."

Wisdom

Be curious. Mistakes and failures can yield opportunities. If you have the right mindset, the opposite of success is not failure—it's learning.

My experience is that great companies begin with these kinds of simple questions:

- "Therefore, what?" This path presents itself when you have an inkling that something is happening. For example, people will own phones with cameras on data networks. Therefore, what will happen is an explosion of photography. Result: Instagram.
- "Is there a better way?" For example, "Is there a better way to sell used goods than garage sales?" "Is there a better

Exhortation

way to gain access to computers than working for a school, government agency, or large company?" Results: eBay and Apple.

- "Isn't this interesting?" Suppose you develop a drug called Sildenafil to treat high blood pressure and angina. It was interesting that trial patients in Swansea, Wales, experienced penile erections. Result: Viagra.

Fried manapua is not as lucrative as Apple or as sexy as Viagra, but if serendipity presents an opportunity, don't be proud. Take it. It doesn't matter how you begin to innovate, only that you do.

Be Nice to Your Interns

In the summer of 1985, I gave a summer job to an undergraduate from USC (the first and last time I helped anyone from USC, because of my Stanford and UCLA pedigree). His task was to write sample assembly-language programs for Macintosh. We provided his programs to Macintosh developers so that they could see how to use this software development path.

Don't worry if you don't know what assembly language is, because it isn't important to the story. This kid was tall, heavy, and fair skinned. He was slightly pushy and obnoxious, as most of us are when we are young, and he was from Hillsborough, one of Northern California's wealthiest areas.

We nicknamed him the Hillsborough Doughboy. In case you're not familiar with the Pillsbury Doughboy, he's the character that jumps out of the Pillsbury Crescent Rolls can in television commercials. He is soft, white, and jovial.

Fast forward a few decades, and the Hillsborough Doughboy started Salesforce.com. Yes, the Hillsborough Doughboy is Marc Benioff. He made billions of dollars, but more telling, he became a generous philanthropist. For example, he donated $200 million to the UCSF hospital system.

The Hillsborough Doughboy grew up to be not only a man, but *The* Man. I like to think I helped his career in a tiny way by giving him that summer job.

And The Man is not just rich and successful, he also has class. In 2015, I emailed him and asked him to help Mike Boich's son get a job at Salesforce.com. Boich was running evangelism in the Macintosh Division and was my boss when Benioff was an intern, so Boich was Benioff's boss's boss. Thirty years later Marc reciprocated by helping Boich's son.

Then, in 2016, I asked Benioff to help my son Nic get a job at Salesforce.com, too, and within three hours of the request, he told his head of global recruiting to get involved. Within a few weeks Nic was a Salesforce employee, so Benioff reciprocated twice to his Apple colleagues from decades earlier.

Most people at Benioff's level would not answer the email, not remember what I had done, or not feel the need to reciprocate. As I said, Benioff has class. And two generations of Kawasakis got their start thanks to nepotism.

Wisdom

Help people indiscriminately. You cannot help too many people. The nerdy punk intern may someday inherit, if not own, the earth. Plus, your kids may need jobs. Also, take the high road and reciprocate to people who have helped you. They may mention you in their book someday.

You can counter this advice and say that it means your time and effort are sub-optimally spent and wasted. For sure this is true, but you will be surprised at how little time and effort on your part can make a world a difference to others.

You're just going to have to trust me on this one.

Make Your Decisions Right

I once watched my daughter, Nohemi, in a longboard surfing competition at Manhattan Beach, California. The conditions were not good for the contest because the waves were short and fast, not affording the kind of long rides that longboards are designed for.

The waves pummeled the contestants, forcing many of them to lose their boards. Several boards, in fact, were broken into pieces, and one contestant broke his ankle by hitting the ocean bottom.

Surfing in general is 90% trying to pick the right place to sit to be in position for the right wave and then taking off at the right time at the right angle and the right speed. There's a big focus on making the right decisions.

At one point, Nohemi was sitting in the absolute wrong place—which is easy for me to say standing on the shore. And she was about to get absolutely crushed by a wave because of where she was sitting. Instead, she turned around a disastrous decision, somehow caught the wave, and got a decent ride, resulting in points from the judges and applause from the crowd.

At that instant, I thought about what Elizabeth Langer, professor of psychology at Harvard and the "mother of mindfulness" dropped in our 2023 interview:

> The way we think we should make decisions is that you know what's going to happen, what's good or bad about different outcomes, you add them up in some complicated way, and then you do what that cost benefit analysis leads you to do.
>
> Wrong! Nobody does it. It doesn't make sense to do it . . .
>
> So what's the bottom line? Since you can't make the right decision, make the decision right.

Wisdom

Decisions in life are rarely clear-cut. It's not enough to just weigh options endlessly and hope for perfection; the real magic happens when you own your choice and work hard to make it right.

It's harnessing a rough patch of uncertainty and shaping it into your victory. This isn't just a piece of advice, it's a mantra for a remarkable life, backed by countless stories of success where adjustment trumped initial choice.

Blowing the Whistle

Tyler Schultz blew the whistle on Elizabeth Holmes and Sonny Balwani, the dynamic duo from Theranos who were convicted of defrauding investors and customers.

When Schultz saw that Theranos's product was ineffective and dangerous while Holmes and Balwani continued to promote it, he took the high road and informed *The Wall Street Journal* and a medical regulator.

This cost him two years of his life, $750,000 in legal fees, and his relationship with George Schultz—his grandfather, company board member, and former US secretary of state.

The obvious question is whether he would do it again. This is what he told me:

> It's an interesting question because when people first started asking me that question when I was twenty-six years old, shortly after, or while I was still really in it, my answer was, "No way, I would never do this again. It was totally not worth it."
>
> And as more and more time has passed, I'm starting to see more the positives that have come out of it, and now that the threats are totally gone, I really have been able to turn this really terrible negative experience into a positive experience.

> . . . I speak to tons of universities and classes, and at conferences, and I really get a lot out of those types of events. I'm always having people coming up to me afterwards saying, "I was in a very similar situation and your story inspired me to do the right thing," and that means a lot to me, it really does.

Wisdom

Often, doing the right thing is neither the simplest nor the most practical option. Nonetheless, remarkableness may be the light at the end of the tunnel. Pay attention to your inner compass and denounce dishonesty and fraud but also recognize that this course involves personal risk.

The Time I Almost Quit Apple

In 1986, I was up for a promotion at Apple. The next level was a directorship—which meant a raise, more stock options, and a company car.

My boss was the chief operating officer of Apple, Del Yocam. In my review he told me that the young, small development businesses loved me. This included companies like Silicon Beach Software, Telos, and T/Maker—places that you probably never heard of.

That was the good news.

The bad news was that three businesses *didn't* like me: Microsoft, Lotus Development, and Ashton-Tate. I was pleased that he knew this, because they were companies that shouldn't have liked me because:

- Microsoft ripped off the Macintosh user interface.
- Lotus created a piece of crap called Jazz.
- Ashton-Tate also created a piece of crap called dBase Mac.

80 Wiser Guy

The review was going so well that I contemplated how big my raise would be and what kind of car to get, but Del didn't see it that way. He thought those three companies were critical for Apple, so I didn't get the promotion.

I was dumbfounded. The enemy of your enemy is your friend, and the friend of your enemy is your enemy, but isn't your enemy your enemy? I was so pissed off that I almost resigned the next day.

Wisdom

Communicate with your boss, so that you know what achievements she's looking for. The rules of the game and the way the score is kept should not surprise you.

Woe unto me because I should have known that Del Yocam wanted me to make the big developers such as Microsoft, Lotus, and Ashton-Tate happy, too. If you think about it, there's no way his perspective could have been "Make the small developers happy and piss off the big ones."

Thus, this debacle was my fault too, and I should have known better than to assume that making small developers happy was enough.

The Time I Did Quit Apple

Within a day of my disappointing meeting with Del Yocam, I saw Jean-Louise Gassée, another executive who reported to Yocam. I told him I was pissed off and was about to quit.

Gassée explained that Apple was reorganizing the management structure, and he would soon be my boss. He went on to say that being a director at Apple was excellent for my resume, so I should stay another six months, and he would promote me to director at my next review.

Exhortation 81

True to his word, he did. However, I resigned on April 1, 1987, the day after my promotion, in order to start a software company called ACIUS with a crazy Frenchwoman named Marylène Delbourg-Delphis, a programmer named Laurent Ribardière, and a product manager named Will Mayall (who became my best friend for life).

At the time, Apple was still fighting the perception that Macintosh lacked software. Rather than solely depending on external developers, it had decided to publish on its own a handful of products such as MacWrite, MacPaint, MacDraw, and 4th Dimension.

Ashton-Tate's dBase, a relational database, was a killer app for the IBM PC. The thinking was that if Macintosh was going to succeed as a business computer, it needed a good relational database. Ashton-Tate didn't believe in Macintosh enough to make a good database for Macintosh.

Meanwhile, Ribardière and Delbourg-Delphis had created 4th Dimension in Paris, and it was a great product, so Apple acquired the publishing rights to it with the intent of making it an Apple-labeled product. When Ashton-Tate found out about Apple's competitive product, the company's CEO went straight to the top and complained to John Sculley, then CEO of Apple.

Sculley, and Yocam caved in and gave 4th Dimension back to Ribardière and Delbourg-Delphis. There was good synergy between Ribardière, Delbourg-Delphis, and me because we all were pissed off with Apple, and we all thought 4th Dimension was a killer product. So we decided to start a company called ACIUS to publish it. I resigned from Apple and became the CEO. The company still exists today.

Another thing happened at ACIUS that changed my life: I wrote my first book, *The Macintosh Way*. Without Delbourg-Delphis's encouragement and faith, I would not have

Wisdom

Quit a job when the timing is optimal, not in a fit of anger. Gassée was right: Having an Apple directorship on my resume was useful for my career because "software evangelist," and later, "software product manager" did not have the gravitas of "director."

Don't quit because of reactionary emotions such as anger and disappointment. Plan your exit. Try to have the next job or opportunity in place. The timing and manner of quitting are just as important as they are when starting a job.

Only Losers Punch Down

Punching down involves belittling, criticizing, or attacking people who have less power, money, or social standing. In the United States, circa 2023, punching down usually occurs against marginalized people: white against Black, male against female, rich against poor, physically abled against physically challenged.

A remarkable example of punching down occurred in 2015 when Donald Trump, at the time the billionaire Republican candidate for the presidency of the United States, made fun of Serge Kovaleski, a reporter who has a disease called arthrogryposis.

This ailment involves multiple joint contractures and deformities. Trump used wild, awkward arm movements to mock Kovaleski at a rally in Myrtle Beach, South Carolina. Trump's desire to humiliate someone in order to get laughs was on full display and a harbinger of behavior to come.

Wisdom

Punching down is for losers. It reflects a lack of grace, class, and intelligence. Remarkable people do not punch down. Clueless, arrogant, insensitive assholes punch down. Be on the right side of this issue. End of discussion.

"I Am Sorry"

In 2023, Paul Sherrell, a Tennessee state legislator, suggested hanging criminals from trees for death penalty sentences:

> I was just wondering, could I put an amendment on that that would include hanging by a tree, also.

Shortly after the shit hit the fan, he issued this apology:

> My exaggerated comments were intended to convey my belief that for the cruelest and most heinous crimes, a just society requires the death penalty in kind. Although a victim's family cannot be restored when an execution is carried out, a lesser punishment undermines the value we place on protecting life.
>
> My intention was to express my support of families who often wait decades for justice. I sincerely apologize to anyone who may have been hurt or offended.

Lisa Leopold, a buddy from the Middlebury Institute of International Studies, is an expert in apologies because she taught a business communication course for international graduate students. This is her review of Paul's apology:

> Grade: D−. Most of this apology reads as a justification for his suggestion (as he expressed "intended" and "intention" twice in the statement).

84   Wiser Guy

There is absolutely no remorse. Calling his comments "exaggerated" hardly captures how offensive they are. The words "I sincerely apologize" are appropriate, but he does not apologize for the transgression but rather for others' (potential) feelings.

There is even a suggestion that there are no victims with the use of hedging in "anyone who may have been hurt or offended." The justification for the transgression, the lack of remorse, the suggestion that there may be no victims, the masking of the seriousness of the offense, and the apology issued only for the potential hurt (rather than the offense) render this apology pretty awful.

Wisdom

The best practice is never to screw up and need to apologize, but that's wishful thinking for all of us. The second best practice is to learn how to apologize well.

I asked Lisa for a list of tips, and this is what she provided:

First, say the words "I am sorry" or "I apologize" to start. Not phrases such as "I never intended," or "It was an accident." Just say you're sorry because the burden is on you to truly apologize.

Second, specify what you did. Otherwise, people won't know what you're sorry about. At an extreme, are you sorry for getting caught, or for what you did? Don't label it as a "mistake," "unfortunate," "bad luck," or "unintentional."

Third, take ownership. Don't qualify your apology by saying, "If I offended or hurt . . ." which implies that if you didn't offend or hurt anyone, you're not sorry. Take ownership. What's important is what the other person thinks, not you.

Fourth, express empathy. Your apology should include an acknowledgment of the damage you caused, and you accomplish this by expressing empathy.

Exhortation 85

I would add one more recommendation about apologies. As with much in life, when it comes to apologies, timing is everything. The longer you wait, the harder it is to apologize, and the more damage the lack of an apology will do.

On the other hand, if you apologize too fast, then the victim can interpret your rush as an attempt to trivialize what happened and quickly move on. My advice is to wait for a moment of sufficient gravitas for your apology.

Change Is Good

Read these two tales of NASA rocket scientists: Mark Rober and Wanda Harding.

Mark began his career at NASA where he worked on the design of the Curiosity rover that went to Mars. On the side, he tinkered with a Halloween costume that used two iPads to simulate seeing through his body. A YouTube video of this costume went viral.

He decided to take a job at Apple shortly after, and he worked on virtual reality in cars. He continued making videos that attracted millions of followers. Ask any Gen Zer about his videos showing thieves opening stolen backpacks and boxes that spray glitter and fart gas, as well as his squirrel Olympics.

He continues to create YouTube videos to interest people in physics, math, and science. He's added a line of scientific toys under the CrunchLabs label. He hopes someday to be a high school physics teacher. His mindset has grown from engineer to evangelist to educator while always being a prankster.

At the end of our interview, he told me this:

> I want to teach in a class. This is what I love about teachers: they're the ultimate investors in human capital. I am the product of some amazing teachers who are themselves products of teachers before them.

> With the teachers, you don't really ever get to see the full impact of your work. But you are investing in people who will then go off and do hopefully amazing things and inspire other folks.

There must be growth-mindset hormones in the water at NASA because Wanda Harding worked there too. She started as a project manager for an electrical contractor. This means she was managing the crew putting wiring into renovated buildings.

She was the senior mission manager at NASA and oversaw the mission that sent the Curiosity rover to Mars. Then she became a technical director at NOAA and oversaw polar orbiting environmental monitoring satellite ground systems.

She has grown from the stars to students because after these careers, she returned to Piedmont College in order to prepare for teaching science to high-need students in Georgia. She shifted from telescope to microscope when she answered a calling to teach science, mathematics, and physics to high school students.

Wisdom

Sometimes you need to embrace change by pursuing new areas outside your comfort zone. Mark and Wanda expanded their mindsets from rocket science into making science videos and teaching high school students, showing how we can grow and make a difference.

Some people find their life calling early. Others jump around. There is no right, optimal way. There is only what works for you and what doesn't.

6 | Observation

Observation more than books and experience more than persons, are the prime educators.

—Amos Bronson Alcott

Observation: a remark, statement, or comment based on something one has seen, heard, or noticed.

How I Became Friends with Jane Goodall

I am friends with Jane Goodall. Let me tell you the story of the fifty-year chain of events that led to this:

1967: My sixth-grade teacher, Trudy Akau, convinces my parents to put me into a college prep school.

1972: I matriculate to Stanford, where I become friends with Mike Boich.

1978: I begin work in the jewelry business and learn how to sell.

1983: Mike hires me into Apple as the second Macintosh software evangelist.

1983–1997: I evangelize Macintosh in various capacities.

2018: Ronit Widman-Levy, executive producer of TEDx Palo Alto, invites me to interview Jane Goodall.

I did not know Ronit. She only knew "of me" because of my work at Apple. Thus, all the dots that led to a career at Apple led to getting Jane Goodall on my podcast.

Wisdom

This story exemplifies how seemingly random events create an interconnected mosaic. A sixth-grade teacher's decision in 1967 set off a fifty-year chain reaction that ultimately connected a tech evangelist with one of the world's most renowned primatologists. Every connection and career choice, no matter how small it seems, can lead to a something good.

The Second Believer Is Key

Derek Sivers created one of the greatest marketing videos of all time. In his TED Talk, Derek showed how a shirtless guy at the 2009 Sasquatch! Music Festival started a movement.

90 Wiser Guy

In it a guy starts solo dancing in the field for what seems like an eternity. Eventually, a second guy joins him. And then a third . . . and pretty soon a crowd of people are dancing. Let's analyze this video:

The "innovator" must be willing to look ridiculous dancing alone on the field.

What the innovator is doing is easy to copy. He's not doing triple axels à la Kristi Yamaguchi.

The first follower transforms the innovator from a nutcase into a leader.

The second follower transforms the innovator and first follower from two nutcases into a group.

The wisdom of the group legitimizes dancing and transforms two nutcases dancing into a crowd activity.

Now let's apply this story to business. In 1984, Apple was trying to break out of the K–12 education and hobbyist market served by the Apple II and sell Macintoshes to businesses. Wishing for something doesn't make it come true, though. On many occasions the press and potential customers asked, "What large companies are using Macintosh?"

Fortunately, there was one: Peat Marwick, now part of KPMG, the accounting and consulting behemoth. Before anyone else, it bought thousands of Macintoshes to increase the efficiency of its field auditors.

When people asked for a "reference account," we would pause for a few seconds as if narrowing down an extensive list and finally say, "Peat Marwick, for example."

The truth was that Peak Marwick was the *only* large company that had adopted Macintosh. This was a fake-it-until-you-make-it, Steve-Jobs-reality-distortion field at its best. The fact that Apple employees believed in Macintosh was nice, but not true

Observation 91

validation. The second believer, like the second dancer, was what mattered.

Wisdom

Derek Sivers's TED Talk illustrates that the first follower is crucial in transforming a lone innovator into a leader, thereby initiating a movement. In business, securing an initial major client, as Apple did with Peat Marwick for the Macintosh, serves as this pivotal first follower, legitimizing the product and encouraging broader adoption.

The Miami LGBTQ+ Canvassers

Geoffrey Cohen, the professor of psychology at Stanford who developed the concept of "good situations" also recommends "wise interventions." He defines this as "interventions that nurture people's belonging and self-worth."

These interventions are brief (ten minutes) and inexpensive but targeted with the intention of long-term behavioral change. He explained the technique to me by citing a study in the Miami-Dade area where canvassers went door to door to discuss transgender rights. The interviews were structured in this way:

Ask open-ended, thought-provoking questions, such as "What do you feel about transgender rights?" to foster discussion.

Listen to people's answers and affirm the validity of their opinions to give them "voice."

Insert "analogic perspective taking," which is the process of calling up a person's own experiences and emotions. For example, the canvassers said, "There's a lot of cases in which people experience the pain of being treated differently just because they're different. Can you think of a time in your life when you had that experience?"

Listen to the shared story when the person was treated differently.

Freeze the experience and lesson. "Given our conversation today, how has it affected your views of transgender rights? Has it changed you in any way? Do you think you'll support it more, support it less, or remain unchanged?"

Geoffrey summarized the results:

> Six months later, they found that these people were much more sympathetic to transgender rights and actually more likely to take a stand against anti-transgender hate propaganda.
>
> I think this is incredibly inspiring, and just goes against this wisdom that people don't change. People do change, but it takes the right kinds of keys.

Wisdom

The wisdom is that a little empathy can spark meaningful change. By listening, validating perspectives, and drawing on people's own experiences, even brief interactions can foster lasting understanding and compassion. Forget the idea that people don't change—with the right "wise interventions," you can unlock the common ground that lies within us all.

The Gorilla Is Invisible

Picture this: You're watching some college students toss balls to each other. There is a team wearing black shirts and a team wearing white shirts. Your task is to count how many times the black team tosses the balls.

Observation 93

This was a cognitive psychology experiment by Dan Simons and Chris Chabris, two research psychologists, in 1999. In the middle of the game a person dressed in a gorilla suit strolls into the scene, beats its chest, and nonchalantly exits. Chabris and Simons found that more than half the time, folks are so focused on counting passes, they completely miss the gorilla's cameo performance.

If you don't believe me, find the video on YouTube and try it on a few people. This experiment is a genius reminder of our human knack for tunnel vision.

Wisdom

The "invisible gorilla experiment" shows our tendency for tunnel vision. When hyper-focused on a task, we can miss the unexpected right in front of us. It's a powerful reminder to stay alert for blind spots and look beyond our immediate focus, because the surprising can happen under our noses.

Keep Your Mouth Shut

If you've ever considered adoption, I strongly encourage it. However, prepare yourself for some strange reactions. For example, shortly before the arrival of Nate, my wife and I had dinner with a friend and his wife. During the meal we told them that we were adopting a second child from Guatemala.

My friend's response, though well-meaning, was "You do know that adopted children tend to have behavioral and learning problems, right?" My unspoken reaction was to what he said was:

> We have already adopted a girl, and I told you we are adopting another child—not just considering adopting again. Your comment is that he's likely to have problems? What kind of asshole are you?

Some men believe that only the fruit of their loins merits parenting. They are idiots. Besides, their typical contribution to a pregnancy is only ten seconds long—five, if they are honest. Having adopted twice, I can tell you that when a caretaker places your baby in your arms at an orphanage, the origin of their DNA doesn't matter.

Wisdom

Don't always express your "honest opinion." My friend's intention might have been good, but did he believe we would cancel the adoption based on his hearsay evidence and opinion? Or return our daughter? Sometimes it's best to just shut up.

Would Elon Do This?

In July 2018, I attended the RISE tech conference in Hong Kong in order to shoot a video with the chair of Mercedes-Benz, Dieter Zetsche, who was giving a keynote speech at the conference. Yes, Dieter and I shot a lot of videos together around the world.

When Zetsche and I sat down for a scene in a Chinese restaurant, the table was rocking. He grabbed a piece of paper, folded it up to the right thickness, and leveled the table. This is the kind of commitment to engineering that you want to see in the company that makes your car.

Would Elon do this? I mean if he has time after running the world. . .

Wisdom

The story of Dieter Zetsche leveling the wobbly table with a folded piece of paper demonstrates the kind of meticulous engineering mindset you want to see in the leader of a company like Mercedes-Benz. It's a reminder not to underestimate the value of that deep commitment to quality and problem-solving.

Finding a Contact Lense in a Pool and a Shark in the Sea

A contact lens once popped out of my eye while I was swimming in my pool, and I decided to try to find it. This wasn't a trivial task, since a residential swimming pool contains approximately 14,000 gallons of water.

My thinking was that because a swimming pool has a finite amount of water, it would be possible to locate the lens. I set off with a small fishnet and spent thirty minutes swimming around like a blue whale sifting out plankton. Believe it or not, I found the lens—though not by using the fishnet.

Instead, I checked the pool filter the next day, and there was the lens. I didn't think it was wise to use that lens again after it had been soaking in chlorinated water for a day, but still, I did find it.

Another story. I used a filter but Dave Ebert is even smarter than me. In July 2023, Madisun and I had lunch with Dave, aka "the shark guy." He's the author of numerous books about sharks, discoverer of more than sixty new species, and TV personality. He regaled us with story after story of studying sharks in South Africa, Sri Lanka, and other exotic places.

At one point he dropped a pearl of a story on us. We thought he goes to these cool places, charters a boat, puts on scuba equipment, dives in, and starts looking.

Nope.

He's much more efficient than that. He goes to fishing villages and checks the catches when the fishing boats come in. "Why should I be one guy in the water looking for sharks when I can see what fifty or sixty boats have caught?"

Dave harnessed the power of complementary people. The probability that your knowledge, skill, time, and energy are all that's needed to make a difference is low. Steve Jobs needed Steve Wozniak at Apple. Melanie Perkins needed Cliff Obrecht and Cameron Adams at Canva. And Dave Ebert needed fishing boats.

96 Wiser Guy

Wisdom

When faced with an impossible task, don't give up. Approach it creatively and think outside the box—there may be a simple, unexpected solution if you're willing to explore different approaches. Persistence and resourcefulness can pay off, even when the odds seem long.

It's smart to find people who complement, not duplicate, your skills and fill in gaps. They have the potential to enhance creativity, decision-making, problem-solving, productivity, and the workplace environment.

Leverage complementary skills and perspectives rather than trying to do everything yourself. By harnessing the collective knowledge and effort of others, you can vastly enhance your own capabilities and impact, just as Dave did by working with local fishing fleets.

Do the Math

In our interview in September 2024, Shalinee Sharma, the CEO of Zearn and author of *Math Mind: The Simple Path to Loving Math*, told me two powerful stories about math.

First, in the 1980s a fast-food chain named A&W decided to go after the McDonald's Quarter Pounder by offering a larger burger. It weighed one-third of a pound instead of McDonald's quarter-pound one.

The promotion failed, and one explanation was that people thought that a Quarter Pounder is larger than a "Third Pounder" because the number four is larger than the number three. But when you divide one pound by three instead of four, it means the A&W burger is larger.

Second, the National Assessment of Educational Progress asked a sample of fourth and eighth graders this question: Which fraction has a value closest to ½?

$$\frac{5}{8}$$

$$\frac{1}{6}$$

$$\frac{2}{2}$$

$$\frac{1}{5}$$

Seventy-six percent of American fourth graders got it wrong. In fact, 41 percent of fourth graders selected the largest, and most incorrect, number ($\frac{2}{2}$) as their answer.

Wisdom

These stories illustrate how a lack of numeracy can lead to significant misunderstandings and poor decisions. If people can't grasp basic fractions, they may think that a quarter is bigger than a third. Hopefully, people would know that a burger weighing 5.3 ounces (⅓-pound) is bigger than a four-ounce (¼-pound) one.

Okay, it's not the end of the world if you pick the smaller burger. It may even be a better dietary choice. But imagine the impact of this lack of math skills when making career, financial, or voting decisions. So learn math yourself. Teach these basic concepts to others. And don't assume that everyone has a sufficient level of proficiency.

What I Learned by Almost Drowning

The Genovese effect is named for Kitty Genovese, a New York City woman who was murdered in 1964. According to the early news reports of her death, thirty-seven or more people heard or may have witnessed her killing and did nothing to stop it.

This led to the development of the social psychology concept called the "bystander effect," which holds that no one takes an action such as calling the police because people assume someone else did.

Subsequent analysis showed that there may have been other factors at work, including that none of the witnesses had seen the entirety of the attack on Genovese. Many later stated that they thought they were overhearing a lovers' quarrel or drunks leaving a bar.

That said, I had an experience along the lines of the Genovese effect. In the summer of 2003, I was bodyboarding with my son Nic at Pajaro Dunes in Watsonville, California, and we were sucked away from the shore by a riptide.

We knew enough to swim parallel to the shore to get out of the riptide, but it's hard to remember what to do when floating all the way to Hawaii is a possible outcome. Before we swam to safety, I screamed for help to several people walking or jogging along the sand.

One jogger looked around to see if we were yelling at him, saw no one else, and yet kept running—God forbid he didn't get his 10,000 steps in that day. This wasn't even the "bystander effect," because there were no bystanders around who he could assume were helping us.

Wisdom

Don't assume that others are helping when you see people in need. I learned that the bystander effect is real. If you are in need yourself, call out to specific people and tell them what to do—for example, "You in the yellow shirt, call the lifeguard!"—and hope they are not as stupid as the guy I encountered.

Small Changes Make a Big Difference

Authors, experts, and organizations love "strategic" decisions that take months and millions of dollars to develop. My experience is that small, simple changes can make big differences in short amounts of time at little expense. History-altering curve jumps are rare, and when they do occur, they start as small changes anyway. Here are three stories that illustrate the power of small changes.

In 2009, the Carrillo Dining Commons on the University of California at Santa Barbara campus stopped providing trays in its all-you-can-eat facility, and food waste declined 40 percent. Trays were still available for parents getting food for kids, but people's behavior changed when it was more difficult to load up with food.

A hospital emergency room was often overcrowded, because indigent people would check in even though they did not need medical attention. All they wanted was a place to sleep. A doctor instituted a practice whereby people had to pay a fee of $0.25 to check in for medical treatment, and the overcrowding stopped. This nominal fee was enough to dissuade people from checking in for medical care that they did not need.

Twenty-five percent of the shipping boxes of the Dutch bike company VanMoof were damaged in transit. The company developed a simple solution: printing the picture of a widescreen TV on the boxes. Damage dropped by 80 percent—apparently because workers care more about damage to TVs than to bikes.

Wisdom

Embrace small changes and "nudges" (in the words of University of Chicago economist Richard Thaler). They can make big differences despite their quick-and-dirty nature.

100 Wiser Guy

My experience is that "clever" almost always trumps "strategic" and expensive changes. You may wonder whether I recommend curve-jumping changes or small ones. The answer is both—and they are not mutually exclusive.

Showing Weakness Is a Sign of Strength

Zatoichi was the name of a blind masseur in a series of Japanese movies. He wandered the countryside minding his own business, but he inevitably wound up righting wrongs with his sword. Think: blind Japanese Robin Hood with a sword.

I saw many Zatoichi movies when I was growing up in Hawaii. This was before the movie industry was concerned about damaging minors with violence and gore, and I guess my parents reasoned that samurai films were part of our culture.

I survived the cinematic trauma, and even learned a valuable lesson. In one movie, as I recall, a criminal gang captured Zatoichi, and the boss of the gang forced him to have sex with a prostitute in front of him and his henchman at a Japanese inn.

The gang members considered Zatoichi weak because he agreed to this humiliation, and they laughed their heads off (literally). Then the innkeeper pointed out that it's difficult for a man to have sex if he's scared—in other words, Zatoichi wasn't scared, so they should be. Shortly after, Zatoichi killed them all.

Wisdom

Don't be afraid to show weakness. Strong people can admit a mistake, change their minds, and tolerate humiliation. Often, this is the first step toward building strength.

Weak people are afraid to show vulnerability. They think this gives their competition the advantage or positions them poorly. Strong people don't see it this way.

Observation 101

When you encounter weakness, flexibility, or the willingness to compromise, don't underestimate your competition and don't overestimate yourself.

When you encounter what appears to be strength, don't overestimate your competition and don't underestimate yourself. In short, be kind, flexible, and humble when you are in a position of strength. This communicates true power better than brute force does.

How I Got My Job at Apple

Most companies rely upon educational background and work experience to determine the acceptability of job candidates. The logic is that employees need a foundation of relevant knowledge and skills to succeed—or at least not make the hiring manager look bad.

But this wasn't how I got my job at Apple. I joined the company in September 1983. On paper (this was before LinkedIn), my resume should not have gotten me an interview. My educational background was a Bachelor of Arts in psychology and an MBA in marketing. I had not taken a computer class—not that there were many computer classes back then.

My work experience was also seemingly irrelevant. After earning my MBA, I went to work for a fine jewelry manufacturer. I started out by counting diamonds and left five years later as vice president of sales and marketing. My only exposure to computers was using an IBM System/32 to enter and access data.

While I was in the jewelry business, my Stanford classmate Mike Boich introduced me to an Apple II, and I fell in love with word processors, spreadsheets, and databases. Word processing in particular was a godsend that was much better than the state-of-the-art IBM Selectric typewriter featuring sticky tape to lift off

102   Wiser Guy

mistakes. Give me AppleWorks, QuickFile, and VisiCalc, and I was ready for anything.

My love of computers inspired me to get a job in the industry, and in early 1983 Mike told me that there was a position in the Macintosh Division to run the Apple University Consortium. This was a program to sell Macintoshes to prestigious universities in order to get their students to use them.

As part of the hiring process, Boich took me into the Macintosh Division building on Bandley Drive in Cupertino and demonstrated MacWrite and MacPaint. When he did, the clouds parted, angels started singing, and I was dumbfounded by how cool Macintosh was.

The Apple University Consortium job was given to someone else, but I was determined to get into the computer industry after the religious experience of seeing a Macintosh. I applied to a dozen computer companies, and I was rejected at each one because I had neither a technical degree nor computer work experience.

My break came in 1982 at Comdex, a computer industry show, in Las Vegas. There I stumbled across a company called Edu-Ware Services, an educational software publishing company in Agoura Hills, California. The person running its sales and marketing, Mike Lieberman, had been injured in a car accident on the way to the show, so there was an opening for which I was hired.

In July 1983, Management Sciences America of Atlanta, Georgia, bought Edu-Ware and placed the company in the Peachtree Software division. The folks at Peachtree tried to convince me to move to Atlanta, but I declined because I couldn't live in a place where sushi was called "bait" and every street was named Peachtree.

Fortunately, Boich contacted me with another opening in the Macintosh Division as a "software evangelist." That position involved convincing software and hardware companies to create Macintosh products. I got the job through nepotism—the

Observation 103

practice of people giving jobs to their friends and relatives—not because of my work or educational background.

My entry into the organization was inauspicious, because Steve Jobs's ringing endorsement was that he liked me, but he wasn't blown away. He told Boich that he could hire me but that he was "betting his job on Guy." I started at Apple in September 1983, and my employee number was 5041.

Wisdom

Relationships are pure gold in the world of opportunities. Job search isn't only about sending out resumes—IMHO, building connections and keeping them warm is more important than perfecting your resume.

This has important ramifications. First, be nice to people so you make friends—I'd even suggest that you be especially nice to the geeks and nerds because they start companies, not the quarterbacks and cheerleaders.

Second, enter at any level. The level you reach matters more than the one where you started. Build on your internship, software tester, database administrator, or receptionist employment.

Third, show a lot of class when you leave a position—even if you're laid off. Don't burn any bridges. You can build an incredible bridge by documenting how to do your job, the current status of important tasks, and crucial upcoming decisions.

Fourth, ignore two considerations when you're doing the hiring 1) the lack of the right background of a candidate who loves your product, and 2) the presence of the right background of a candidate who doesn't.

How I Passed Up the Most Lucrative Job of My Career

A short time after Yahoo! started in 1995, venture capitalist and startup empire-maker Michael Moritz asked me if I wanted to apply for the CEO position. He was on Yahoo!'s board of directors as a representative of Sequoia Capital, one of the company's lead investors.

At the time, my wife, Beth, our son Nic, and I lived in San Francisco on Union Street in a house with well-trimmed bougainvillea, and Yahoo!'s offices were an hour's drive away in light traffic. My wife was also in beta with our second son, Noah, so we were about to have a two-year-old and a newborn.

I told Moritz that I didn't want to interview for the job because it meant two hours of driving every day, and I couldn't see how the company could make money. Yahoo! was then nothing more than a collection of the cofounders' favorite websites.

FYI, over the course of its operation, Sequoia's investments had achieved a public-market value of $1.4 trillion, so turning down this interview was foolish—at least in hindsight.

This was the costliest mistake I've made in my career. As I'm writing this book, I've revisited this decision for approximately twenty-eight years, thirty days, eight hours, and fifteen minutes. Here's how I look at it:

- If I had interviewed, I probably would have gotten the job.
- My stock option package would have amounted to 5 percent of the company.
- Yahoo!'s market capitalization peaked at $100 billion in the 2000 timeframe.
- 5 percent of $100 billion is $5 billion.

Let's say my calculation is off by 50 percent. This still means I lost $2.5 billion. And $2.5 billion here and $2.5 billion there adds up to real money. The question I've been asking myself ever since is "Why was I so stupid?"

Observation 105

I have no regrets about choosing to spend time with my wife and kids, but what pisses me off about my decision is my stupidity:

- I thought that the Internet was nothing more than an extension of personal computers—it was simply what was coming through the Macintosh modem cable. It wasn't a new industry.
- I didn't even meet with a world-famous venture capitalist from a world-famous firm after they asked me if I was interested in a job.
- I wasn't smart enough to understand that companies morph. Yahoo! may have started as a directory of the Internet, but it morphed into email, commerce, search, photography, and so much more.

Wisdom

For $2.5 billion, I damn well better have gained some wisdom. You be the judge of whether these lessons are worth it. First, you can't put a price tag on being there for your family, even if you missed Yahoo!'s rocket ship ride.

Second, you never know how a business may morph on its way to success—if only we all had a crystal ball. In the end, while I kick myself for not foreseeing the future, I'm glad I embraced my present.

How I Got My Job at Canva

In March 2014, Peg Fitzpatrick, my co-author on *The Art of Social Media*, was posting my tweets. She used a product called Canva to create graphics for them. The folks at Canva noticed that I used it and reached out to me via Twitter.

I wasn't sure what Peg was using for my tweets, so I had to verify with her that Canva was indeed it. I also had to ask her if I should help the company. A few weeks later, Melanie Perkins and Cliff Obrecht, two of the three cofounders of Canva, and Zach Kitschke, the company's marketing guy, were in the United States, so we met at my house.

I liked them and what they were trying to do: democratize design. And they had a good story: Perkins was an instructor at the University of Western Australia and noticed that Adobe Illustrator and Photoshop were too hard to learn and too expensive to buy. Within a few weeks of our meeting, I signed on as Canva's chief evangelist.

Fast forward to 2025, and Canva is valued at $40 billion. (A billion-dollar valuation is the threshold for becoming a "unicorn.") Though it's lofty territory, such a valuation is no guarantee of success, and the value of stock options is not the same as real money.

But it's a lot better to own stock options in a unicorn than not. This is what had to happen to for me to become the chief evangelist of Canva:

- Peg had to find, use, and like Canva. Then she had to use it for my Twitter account, not only her own.
- Perkins, Obrecht, or Kitschke had to follow me on Twitter and notice that I was using their product.
- One of them had to tweet a message to me.
- I had to notice the tweet. This isn't as simple as it sounds, because hundreds of people were mentioning me in their tweets back then.
- I had to respond to their tweet in a manner that started a conversation.

Observation 107

- They had to be in the United States shortly thereafter—because I'm not known for my attention span and recollection of social media encounters.

If you multiply the probability of each step to derive the overall likelihood of me joining Canva, the number is close to zero. In other words, I became the chief evangelist because of a humongous amount of good fortune and serendipity!

Wisdom

First, listen to the people you work with. They probably know more than you do. Without Peg, I would not have become the chief evangelist of Canva. Lots of things had to align for me to work for a company like Canva, but it all started with her.

Second, take chances. There was no guarantee that Canva would become such a success. After the fact, people like to say they "knew" something would succeed, but this is selective memory and reality distortion. How many times did they know something that didn't come true?

Third, get ready for a marathon. Starting a company is not a sprint. It's not as simple as creating a product, selling it, and cashing out. Entrepreneurship is a marathon combined with decathlon—that is, you have to do a lot of things well for a long time.

The Beauty of the Performative

The word "performative" refers to actions or expressions that enact or accomplish something by the very act of being performed. They are things of beauty, and here are four stories to illustrate how they work.

108 Wiser Guy

First, Steve Jobs was a master of it. For example, he used the phrase "one more thing" to signal that he was about to unveil something special.

1999: Introduction of the AirPort wireless networking system
2000: Unveiling of the Power Mac G4 Cube
2001: Launch of the Titanium PowerBook G4
2003: Debut of the Power Mac G5
2004: Reveal of the iPod mini in various colors
2005: Announcement of the iPod shuffle
2006: Introduction of the MacBook Pro
2010: Launch of FaceTime video calling
2011: Presentation of iTunes Match

Second, when making in-person speeches, I often show up with my own Countryman E6 microphone. This mic is renowned for its high fidelity, compact size, and light weight.

I know that there is probably a very good audio setup and crew. They have the best equipment—including mics that are Countrymans or equal. But when you show up with your own, you are sending a message: "I really care about how I sound. I am not leaving it to chance." And the audio crew is impressed and takes better care of you.

Third, go listen to my podcast. The first question usually seems to come out of left field—in other words, strange if not weird. So much so that your initial reaction may be "What the hell is Guy talking about?" It's out of left field for you, but the guest knows exactly what I'm talking about.

The performative aspect of this practice is to signal that I am deeply prepared for this interview, and it's not the kind of interview where a producer handed the host a Wikipedia entry a minute before.

Observation 109

For example, the first question I asked Neil deGrasse Tyson in our interview was why his son is named Travis since his daughter is named Miranda, after one of the moons of Uranus. He had four other moons he could have used: Ariel, Umbriel, Titania, and Oberon.

Fourth, always take notes in meetings—even if you don't need the notes and will not use them. (You might be surprised that you do.) For one thing, the act of writing down notes help you remember things. But the performative value is that when people see you take notes, they think that you are diligent, attentive, and intelligent—in other words, "She's so smart she took notes when I talked."

Wisdom

Performative actions aren't just about showing off; they can be strategic moves that demonstrate deep preparation, attention to detail, and mastery of your craft. When you execute these moves correctly, like Jobs's "one more thing" or bringing your own mic to a speech, you're not just doing something—you're sending a powerful signal that shapes how people perceive and respond to you.

Michelle Obama's Hair

In 2020, I got into a discussion about the hairstyles of Black women with Julie Lythcott-Haims, an author, speaker, Palo Alto City Council member, and former dean at Stanford. Her conclusion was "it's on us as Black women to wear the hair that makes us feel beautiful and proud."

The interview was the day after Michelle Obama had spoken at the 2016 Democratic National Convention. Her hair had been pressed, so I asked Julie what to make of that. My thinking was that of all Black women in the world, Michelle Obama could wear her hair "natural" or any other way she wanted.

110 Wiser Guy

Here's Julie's response:

> There are a lot of folks still even in her intended audience, the Democratic Party, who would see a Black woman wearing her hair natural as being inappropriate. They would see it as less professional and not what it quote-unquote "should be." I think Michelle Obama knows that.
>
> So when she is asked to ascend to an important podium and give one of the greatest speeches of her life, she's probably being very strategic and thinking, "Today is a day for pressed hair because that will be what will allow me to be heard by the most people."

There's no doubt that complex and nuanced conversations about issues such as Black women's hair reveal important societal expectations and biases. However, weigh these issues against the message that you wish to convey and the impact you seek.

Wisdom

The key takeaway here is the importance of strategic decision-making in communication. Michelle Obama's choice wasn't about self-expression that day but about ensuring her message reached the widest audience. Recognize the landscape you're navigating, and sometimes adapt to ensure your voice is heard, even if it means bending societal norms temporarily.

Ignoring Is Bliss

A large European company sent a contingent of its top executives to Silicon Valley in 2017. The goal was to learn about entrepreneurship, innovation, and the "Silicon Valley" way—as if we have magical pixie dust here, but that's another story.

Observation 111

I was the first person with whom they met, and my role was to provide an introduction to the region. After my presentation, we went outside and posed for a group picture behind a Mercedes-Benz.

I posted the picture to Facebook and LinkedIn, generating much engagement. So far, so good—a win-win for me, because I was a Mercedes-Benz brand ambassador, and a win for the company, because it depicted its employees learning about innovation in Silicon Valley.

However, one random person on LinkedIn expressed surprise that the company allowed me to post a picture containing a brand that the company did not sell. Based on one observation, despite dozens of likes and positive comments by others, the company asked me to remove the picture.

Wisdom

Sweat the big stuff and ignore the chatter—especially on social media. After all I had told them about believing anything is possible, getting to the next curve of innovation, forgiving failure, and hating bureaucracy, the company was leery of a picture of its employees behind a product it didn't sell.

I found this ironic. The company went through so much expense and trouble to expose its managers to Silicon Valley but couldn't cope with a single comment. And that comment wasn't even negative. Compared to the challenges that companies face, this one was inconsequential.

Unveil Your Passions

In the late 1980s, I spoke at the Pentagon Mac Users Group at, logically, the Pentagon. Major Steve Broughall had started the group to help people in the military use Macintoshes. During

112 Wiser Guy

my speech, I joked that I would trade a Macintosh II (then the most sought-after model) for a ride in a fighter jet.

Somehow the commander of the Alaskan Air Command learned what I had said and invited me to fly in an F-15E at the Elmendorf Air Force Base in Anchorage, Alaska. So I went to Anchorage, because riding in a fighter jet is a rare experience for anyone—military or civilian.

The best amusement park ride in the world is nothing compared to flying in a fighter jet. It was a long, involved, and mind-altering experience:

- There were four hours of briefing and preparation to get to the point of taking off.
- I received at least five warnings about the danger of pulling the ejection lever.
- I could barely move in the cockpit. I was scared shitless the whole time and about to throw up, too.
- When the plane made a sharp turn, it felt like I was in a towel that God was wringing out.

I don't know how fighter pilots fly, attack, and evade at the same time. It was difficult to just sit there. The pilot let me take the stick once, and it was the most power that's ever been between my legs.

Then, to top it off, an Alaskan volcano erupted (I think it was the Mount Redoubt eruption of 1989) the day after the flight, and all airlines were grounded, so I was stuck in Alaska for a few days. The ground was covered with ash. The semi-apocalyptic ending to this experience was just perfect.

But wait, there's more. I wrote a *Macworld* magazine column about this amazing adventure in which I mentioned the joke about trading a Macintosh II for a ride. Someone who read the

Observation 113

article took it seriously and reported my "bribe" to the inspector general of the US Air Force.

One day I got a call from an investigator from the inspector general's office and had to do some fast talking to keep the commander and me out of trouble. There's a file about my investigation somewhere in the Air Force archives—one day I may try to get it via the Freedom of Information Act.

Wisdom

Make your personal interests known. This provides "hooks" to develop additional and deeper relationships. Don't broadcast anything prurient, illegal, or controversial, but showing the non-business side of yourself is a powerful way to make you more interesting and approachable. And doing so can create opportunities for adventures such as flying in a fighter plane.

I'm not sure if there's any wisdom to garner from being investigated for bribing the general. I certainly didn't bribe him, and if I had to do it all over again, I would do it all over again for sure!

7 | Innovation

If you always do what you've always done, you'll always get what you've always got.

—Henry Ford

Innovation: a new method, idea, product, or the like.

You Are the Customer

The "creating what you want to use" method for driving innovation wasn't invented or perfected by tech nerds. One of my favorite stories of alleviating pain involves Bette Nesmith Graham, inventor of Liquid Paper in the early 1950s. Bette was a secretary in a Texas bank and wanted a way to correct her typing mistakes.

She experimented with various paints and soap and then added titanium dioxide to her formulas. The concoction covered up mistakes completely, and soon other secretaries asked her for her correction fluid, and liquid paper was born.

We hear more about the ideas that succeeded and less about the ideas that failed (remember to think about what's missing). But when you create something for yourself, there is at least one person who desires it, and you are in the game.

Wisdom

Alleviating your own pain is about fixing something in your life and turning it into opportunities for innovation. Bette experienced the pain of correcting mistakes and created a solution.

By focusing on pain, she not only solved immediate issues but transformed the experience into something truly useful. Woz made the computer he wanted to use. Mark Zuckerberg, reportedly, needed help finding dates. This approach underscores that the key to success is often buried in the challenges people face every day.

Go and Be

Toyota extols the principle of *genchi genbutsu* (go and see for yourself). For Toyota that means that one should go and see what's happening on the factory floor, in car dealers, and in the lives of customers as they use cars.

118 Wiser Guy

This process helps you gain an appreciation of what people are experiencing to improve their lives with innovations. For example, seeing how a young family deals with a baby, stroller, dog, and siblings influenced the design of Toyota's minivans.

Even better than going and seeing is the concept of *taiken gakushuu* (experiential learning). Doing or participating is the way to learn. For example, a large pharmaceutical company asked Martin Lindstrom, Norwegian psychologist and executive leader, to help the company "get closer to the customer."

Usually, this involves focus groups and surveys. Instead, he assembled the executives in a room and made them breathe through straws. Many executives thought this was a waste of time, and most had difficulty doing it for more than a few minutes.

At the end of the exercise, Martin asked the participants if they now understood what it's like to be someone with asthma. These executives didn't simply go see or imagine themselves as asthmatic. They *experienced* what it's like to have asthma, not just watch people with asthma.

Wisdom

The core lesson here is that true understanding comes from direct experience, not just observation. Toyota's *genchi genbutsu* highlights the importance of seeing real conditions, but *taiken gakushuu* takes it up a notch by immersing oneself in the customer's reality.

It's about transcending reports and data to forge real empathy by walking a mile in your customer's shoes—breath by breath, through a straw, if necessary.

What Does the Cow See?

Another "go and be" story. When Temple Grandin, professor, animal behaviorist, and visual thinker, was a graduate student at Arizona State University, she figured out why cattle would balk at walking through chutes.

Innovation 119

While the ranch hands resorted to prodding, pushing, and yelling, she got down into the chute and "became" a cow. She saw the shadows, rays of light, and distractions to understand what made the cows hesitate. *Yellowstone* fans: I ask you, "Doesn't this seem like something John Dutton would do?"

"Go and see" and "go and be" foster the ability to feel what other people are feeling. This is a good practice. However, being remarkable requires making the leap from empathy to action. The desire to relieve what's causing suffering is called compassion.

For example, it's great that you now realize that senior citizens can't open their bottles of pills or that breathing through straws is a pain in the ass, but what are you going to do for them? Empathy is a visceral reaction. Compassion is a conscious action.

And, to quote Jordan Kasalow, the author of *Dare to Matter: Your Path to Making a Difference*: "Now, while empathy can exhaust us, compassion nourishes us. It does not cost us anything. The more we contribute, the more it will grow." So one path to remarkableness is to go see, go be, or go do.

Wisdom

Empathy guides you to understand another's perspective and then to find compassion that drives change. Temple shows us this by literally stepping into the perspective of cattle, identifying their fear sources, and acting on it. This story isn't just about seeing but turning empathy into compassion—action that resolves suffering they're facing.

There's a direct correlation between understanding deeply and innovating powerfully, whether in business or in personal life. Consider how businesses draw closer to their customers through experiential learning. By walking in their shoes, companies unveil unique insights that prompt meaningful changes.

120   Wiser Guy

Work Backwards

According to Colin Bryar, former chief of staff of the founder and CEO of Amazon, one of the keys to Amazon's success was the practice of creating new products and services by working backwards from what customers wanted.

Kodak is the mother of bad examples of this concept. In 1970, a Kodak engineer named Steven Sasson invented the digital camera. His invention weighed eight pounds and had a resolution of 100×100 pixels. (An iPhone 14 weighs six ounces and has a resolution of 2556×1179 pixels.)

Unfortunately, Kodak lived and died on the film curve. In case you don't know what film is, it's a sheet of plastic covered with chemicals designed to "capture" a picture when exposed to light. Once exposed, you would take your roll of film to a lab or drugstore for processing. In as little as an hour or as long as a few days, you could see your pictures.

Kodak did not embrace the next curve of photography even though it invented digital photography. It must have thought it was a chemical and film company. I would guess things didn't go well when Steve told his management that he invented a product to make the company's current products unnecessary!

This is a classic example of a fixed mindset. Kodak apparently defined its business as a packager of film and chemicals— that's what it did, the business was lucrative, and it wasn't going to change.

If it defined its business as the preservation of memories and jumped the curve from chemicals to digital chips, we might be using Kodak cameras today, and its technology would be in every phone. In other words, what Sony is, circa 2025.

Wisdom

Kodak's downfall teaches us the danger of clinging to an outdated vision when the future's knocking at the door. By failing

Innovation 121

to shift from chemicals to digital innovation, Kodak missed its chance to lead the photography revolution. Remember, visionaries work backwards from the customer, not from the bottom line, to jump on the next big thing.

Reebok's White Space

Joe Foster, the founder of Reebok, told me this story of "looking for white space." When the company arrived in America in 1979, it made only running shoes. But then an employee named Arnold Martin saw that his wife was loving classes where people were "exercising to music."

Arnold went to the next class and saw the instructor and half the students in sneakers. The other half was not wearing shoes. This inspired Arnold to want to make aerobics shoes for women. Arnold got 200 samples made, and they sold immediately.

Arnold had helped Reebok develop a product that was unique and valuable that filled a profitable white space because no other company was making shoes for women to wear while doing aerobics. And then Jane Fonda wore a pair and helped propel Reebok from a $9 million company into a $900 million company.

Wisdom

If you offer something unique and valuable, then marketing, selling, fundraising, and recruiting all get easier—it is the holy grail, the promised land of innovation, so do your best to create products and services that embody both qualities.

Establish a Subcategory

David Aaker, the godfather of branding, told me that creating an entirely new category is often too hard and too late. Establishing a subcategory is remarkable enough.

122 Wiser Guy

Think about how much more difficult it would be for Tesla if it had tried to introduce a new mode of transportation instead of an electric *car*. Or GoPro to introduce a new kind of device instead of an action *camera*. Or Kindle to introduce a new kind of device instead of an e-reader *tablet*.

It's cheaper to create a niche within a category because people have a basic understanding of what you do. It is easier to explain a Kindle e-reader as a subcategory of tablets than as a totally new market.

You can target groups with unique needs and requirements. This helps you focus your efforts and easily ignore other segments. GoPro, for example, doesn't have to worry about serving wedding photographers unless the wingsuit wedding suddenly takes off.

You can redefine and reposition your competitors. For example, an electric-car company can label its internal combustion competitors as brands that don't care about the environment.

While you cannot discourage competitors in a large, generic market, by creating a subcategory you can encourage them to leave you alone. Have you heard of action cameras made by Sony, Canon, Leica, or Nikon? That's because they all leave GoPro alone.

Wisdom

Creating a new category is a remarkable accomplishment, but new categories are rare. You can make a difference without completing this monumental endeavor. I want you to envision yourself as a large fish in a large pond, and this you can do by starting with a subcategory.

What Do "Experts" Know?

Don't accept that what everyone "knows" is true. Primatologists thought they "knew" that chimps were vegetarians with limited

Innovation 123

social interactions, and they believed that only humans have the intelligence to create and use tools.

Back in the 1960s, mainstream science had rigid ideas about animal behavior, seeing humans as separate from the natural world. This was widely believed until Jane Goodall asked the experts, "How do you know chimps aren't social?"

As the Bible says, "Out of the mouth of babes and sucklings hast thou ordained strength." Posing questions that lack guile and come from a place of innocence, naivete, or candidness is a rich vein for ideas to make the world a better place.

Rather than take the word of experts, many of whom never studied chimps in the field, Jane went and observed the chimps in their natural habitat. She observed chimps using tools, something previously thought unique to humans. They formed long-term relationships, engaged in affectionate gestures like kissing and embracing, and displayed a wide range of emotional expressions and social bonds.

Wisdom

Jane's legacy reminds us of the power in questioning "established truths" and embracing a multiplicity of perspectives. In pushing boundaries and challenging assumptions, we open the door to breakthrough insights—a crucial lesson for anyone, whether you're an entrepreneur, a leader, or an innovator in your field.

Embrace curiosity, challenge norms, and create a path forged by personal discovery rather than preconceived ideas. These are the tools of a revolutionary thinker. Are you ready to embrace them and question what you think you know? Let's keep questioning and discovering.

Prove Your Concept

The goal of proving your concept is what education guru Ken Robinson calls "the transition from imagination to creation."

124   Wiser Guy

People have watched his TED Talk called "Do Schools Kill Creativity?" over sixty million times, and Queen Elizabeth II knighted him for his work. This is how he explained the process to me:

> Imagination is the capacity we all have, we're born with it as human beings, to bring into mind things that aren't present to our senses. To transcend the here and now, to anticipate the future, to reflect on the past, to step outside, to speculate, to ask, "What if?"
>
> It's not a single power. It's an amalgam of many powers that we have, but the ability to bring to mind things that aren't present is the root of it. Creativity is a step on from that. It's putting your imagination to work. It's applying it in some specific way.

The most perilous proof of concept that I've heard of was by Chris Bertish. He's the first person to solo paddle across the Atlantic Ocean. It took him ninety-three days, and he was self-sufficient without a support boat.

His proof of concept that this was possible was a solo paddle from Cape Point to Lambert's Bay, a 350-kilometer (217-mile) journey through cold, turbulent, shark-infested waters along the west coast of South Africa. Think about that as a proof of concept. Sure puts creating a pitch or sending a file to a 3D printer to shame.

Wisdom

The heart of Ken's and Chris's lessons is the alchemy of mind and action. Imagination is only the spark, and creativity is what turns that spark into reality.

Innovation 125

By doing a proof of concept, you can learn that your idea is possible, figure out ways to make it better, garner external support as people see your idea in action, and build your self-confidence.

So don't just imagine, create.

Make a Bigger Pie

This is technical jargon for creating products and services that other organizations can supplement with features and functionality. This enables other organizations not only to buy into your dreams, but also to integrate their products into your dreams too.

For example, when Sony introduced its Alpha series of mirrorless cameras, an initial weakness was the lack of different lenses. Sony did not have the resources to create both new cameras and also all the necessary lenses.

However, Sony supported the efforts of other companies to create compatible lenses, and by 2023 the availability of Sony-compatible lenses from companies such as Tamron and Sigma became a reason to buy a Sony camera and not a Canon or Nikon camera.

However, an open architecture involves extra work and a commitment to the big picture:

Sharing the pie in the pursuit of baking a bigger pie (Sony is foregoing revenue from lens sales by allowing Tamron and Sigma to sell Sony-compatible lenses)

Documenting how your product or service works at its root level so that others can understand it too and make compatible products

Providing support to external parties as they come up to speed with the technical requirements for building compatible products

There is also an argument for a closed architecture. In this scenario, a camera manufacturer would not enable any other products to work with its camera—maximizing its own revenue. Controlling the system can mean better integration and a smoother customer experience.

I favor an open architecture but either method can work. And both at the same time can work too. Apple's computers, for example, are "closed" to most hardware changes, but the iOS and Macintosh app stores are "open" to application developers.

Thousands of applications created by these developers have increased the functionality of Apple's products. My experience at Apple taught me that an open architecture is an effective method for recruiting others to your team, evangelizing your vision, and achieving success.

Wisdom

The beauty of open architecture is inviting collaboration to elevate your product and expand your ecosystem. Sony's strategy with the Alpha series illustrates how empowering others to contribute can multiply your impact and convert competitors into valuable partners.

Ultimately, this approach fuels innovation and broadens your market reach, creating a win-win scenario for all involved.

Be a Mission-Driven Asshole

Do I need to tell you any more about Tony Faddell than that he created the iPod, iPhone, and Nest thermostat? These inventions are three of *Time's* "50 Most Influential Gadgets of All Time." If you had created one, you'd be doing great. If you created three, that's a trend, and you're remarkable.

In 2022, Tony published a book called *Build: An Unorthodox Guide to Making Things Worth Making*, in which he makes the

Innovation 127

case for mission-driven asshole CEOs. According to Tony, there are four kinds of assholes:

Political: These people are concerned with surviving and making themselves look good by sucking up. They also work behind the scenes to undermine others.

Controlling: These are the micromanagers who are threatened by talented people. No one else has good ideas except them, and they seek to control even the minutia of the workplace.

Ego-driven: This is the purest form of asshole: mean, crude, manipulative, defensive, and angry. You would cross the street to avoid saying hello to them.

Mission-driven: Dedicated to the mission of the organization, they steamroll people who aren't excellent. They care a lot. They work hard. They listen and change their minds if you are right. Steve Jobs was this type of asshole.

This is what Tony told me about working for Steve and what it means to be a mission-driven asshole:

He wasn't an ego-driven asshole, not at least from what I can see. He cared that the mission was right and right on.

You don't judge the people. You judge and critique the work that those people do. You make sure that you're doing it in support of what's going to be the best for the customer and educating.

But you're going to be relentless. You're going to make sure that the team just doesn't take second best. They go find the best. Literally drive every single one of the details that matter.

128 Wiser Guy

Unfortunately, running an organization is not unicorns farting pixie dust while singing "Kumbaya." Sometimes you must push your team with rough love.

You may need to send back mediocre work for improvement, perhaps several times, until you decide it cannot be better. You may appear to be an asshole to them.

This is better than your team thinking you're a pushover who doesn't expect greatness. Why you're a jerk matters. For your ego? To conceal insecurities? Or because you want their finest work and career success?

I know no Macintosh Division employee who didn't believe Steve Jobs was a jerk. I don't know anyone from the Macintosh Division who didn't think working under Steve was an honor and privilege, and we'd do it again if we could.

Wisdom

A critical takeaway from Tony Fadell's insights is that leadership demands a relentless focus on the mission over ego. The power lies in being a "mission-driven" leader, not a tyrant, and valuing excellence and pushing teams beyond their comfort zone to achieve remarkable results.

Doing this isn't always rainbows and sunshine, but if done with integrity, it can transform good work into groundbreaking innovation that resonates across time.

The Law of Big Numbers

Behind my house there was a hill covered with eucalyptus trees. Many things that I love come from Australia, including Canva (online design), Cochlear (cochlear implant), Rode (podcast equipment), and Espresso (portable monitors), but eucalyptus trees are not one of them.

Innovation 129

Scientists estimate that they use several hundred liters of water per day, and they are highly flammable because of their oil content. They also shed their bark, which adds to the supply of combustible material.

You can't even trim some tree species in California, but it's open season on eucalyptus trees. I had the hill wiped clean of this invasive species by removing 300 of them. (If you want eucalyptus chips or wood, let me know.)

Then, faced with a denuded hill, my challenge was to repopulate it with a native species such as oaks. These are beautiful trees that provide an ecosystem for caterpillars, birds, and other animals. Plus they also help water infiltrate the soil.

Having become stoked about oaks, I came to learn that growing oaks is a nontrivial task. In many ways, this process is a model for personal growth and preparation for a remarkable life. For one thing, I had to face my mortality: I may never sit under the shade of any of these trees because of my age.

The gist of the process for populating a hill is this:

Gather hundreds of acorns from the ground beneath existing trees. These are free, abundant, and barely noticed by most people. University Avenue in downtown Los Gatos, California, is a good place to look if you live in the San Francisco Bay Area.

Identify the bad acorns by dropping them in water. If they float, they are rotten or dead. If they sink, they are healthy. (The analogy to life breaks down a little here.)

Place them in a refrigerator in moist material or under damp paper towels for a month or two. This is called stratification—it simulates the exposure to cold that acorns experience in the wild that prepares them for germination.

Plant them an inch below the surface in pots or in the field. Water and feed them. Watch what happens and eliminate

130 Wiser Guy

the weak ones. Most will not sprout. Forget "plug and play." My mantra is "plant and pray."

Transfer the seedlings from pots into the soil. Be sure not to disturb the root structure. Protect them from animals with a wire fence or plant tube.

Water and feed them, then wait for ten to twenty years. Then behold what a magnificent tree can grow from a tiny seed.

Three years later, there are only two viable saplings from the several hundred acorns that started the process. The metaphor of planting acorns is perfect for the growth mindset. That is, you must collect, prepare, plant, tend, and wait. It is as simple to describe as it is difficult to accomplish.

Wisdom

Clearing the hill of eucalyptus trees was more than landscaping; it was a masterclass in resilience and vision. Planting oaks is a metaphor for life's challenges, where you nurture potential and trust the process despite uncertainty.

It's about investing in a future you might not see, embracing deliberate patience, and never underestimating the power of humble beginnings to yield grand results.

Letting Flowers Bloom

This is a line stolen from Chairman Mao Zedong, although I fail to see how he implemented it. My advice is to let any kind of flower blossom and be thankful that anything blossoms at all.

For example, in 1984 Apple intended Macintosh to become a spreadsheet, word processing, and database computer. Apple went zero for three as the IBM PC remained the go-to computer for these functions. Instead Aldus and Adobe, two software startups, created software that enabled people to use Macintoshes to publish books, magazines, and newspapers.

Innovation

131

I learned to be thankful that your seeds took root and sprouted plants of any kind. To return to my acorns and oaks metaphor, it's as if I planted acorns but wind-dispersed maple seeds landed on my hill and took root. Works for me!

Here are more examples of seeds that blossomed in unintended ways:

Name	Intended Use	Actual Use
Viagra	Treatment of angina and high blood pressure	Treatment of erectile dysfunction
Bubble wrap	Textured wallpaper	Protective packaging
Play-Doh	Wallpaper cleaner	Children's toy
Slinky	Spring for naval equipment	Children's toy
Duct tape	Waterproofing ammunition cases	Everything

The way this works is that you do your best to create a great product or service, take your best guess at positioning it, and then see what happens. Maybe you were right all the way along, but be prepared for surprises at who adopts your product or service and what they do with it.

Then "take the sale" and be humble. Do things to increase the satisfaction of your early adopters and establish a foothold with them. Then proceed to other markets and industries.

Wisdom

The lesson here is that innovation is messy, unpredictable, and full of delightful surprises. You might aim for one thing and end up with something entirely different, but that's part of the thrill. And it should even be part of an intentional strategy!

Be grateful for what blossoms, even if it's not what you originally planted—because the market often shapes your destiny in unexpected ways.

8 | Salvation

Do your little bit of good where you are; it's those little bits of good put together that overwhelm the world.

—Desmond Tutu

Salvation: preservation or deliverance from harm, ruin, or loss.

The Memorial Mindset

From 2010 to 2019, Carol Dweck and I traveled around the world to deliver speeches. I gave fifty to seventy-five per year. She may have given more. When people asked me where I wrote during those years, my answer was "United Club."

We both lived thirty miles from San Francisco International Airport, and we happened to use the same limousine service run by a nice guy named Chris Webster. He was a one-man show—no website, no fleet of Mercedes-Benzes—just Chris and one old Lincoln Town Car.

He drove rich and famous Silicon Valley entrepreneurs, executives, and venture capitalists as they strove to achieve worldwide domination. (If you want to learn more about these moguls, check out Chris's book, *Confessions of a Chauffeur*.)

Alas, Chris died in 2019, and on Sunday, April 7, 2019, there was a memorial service for him at the Unity Palo Alto church. I attended the service with my son Nate. It was a small affair of fifty people—no Bono or Norah Jones or Al Gore—just friends and family.

But Carol Dweck was there with her husband.

Which is to say that of the hundreds of people Chris had picked up at 5:00 a.m., waited for after midnight, and drove on holidays and weekends for years, only Carol Dweck was there. I was already in love with her work, but when I saw her at Chris's funeral, she ascended to the top of people I admire.

She wanted to honor Chris and did not view him as merely "a driver" in her address book. She truly is a gracious person, and I hope this story will help you embrace her gospel of the growth mindset. You can tell a lot about a person by what they do when there's no money or glory involved.

Wisdom

True character isn't revealed in keynote speeches or bestselling books—it shows up at a humble driver's funeral when nobody's watching. Carol Dweck doesn't just teach the growth mindset; she lives it by treating everyone, from CEOs to chauffeurs, with equal respect and genuine care. This is the kind of authenticity that separates the real deal from the Silicon Valley pretenders and billionaire robber barons.

Money from Out of the Blue

Jacob Martinez is the director of Digital NEST, an organization that helps Hispanic youth in Watsonville, California, develop alternate career paths to working in agricultural fields. In mid-2023, he texted me to tell me he had some good news.

Indeed he did. Yield Giving was about to support Digital NEST by donating over $1 million to the organization. Wow! Yield Giving is the foundation set up by MacKenzie Scott, the ex-wife of Amazon founder Jeff Bezos.

This is how the text conversation went between Jacob and me:

> **Guy:** Wow. Those books and DVDs sure added up!!! Was it a nightmare to get through her screening?
>
> **Jacob:** We didn't even apply. Her team said they have been following our work and that she was really impressed. We did a short interview and then got a call a few months later.

In addition to not having to apply, there are no reporting requirements and rules attached to the grant. MacKenzie is saying, "We like what you're doing. We trust you. Go do it." This is a remarkable example of gracious giving.

Salvation

Fast-backward five decades to when I was in college. My father explained the concept of noblesse oblige to me. It is the understanding that with privilege comes responsibility and obligation.

My term is "success oblige"—meaning that anyone and everyone who is successful has moral responsibilities and obligations. MacKenzie Scott is a great example. However, you don't have to be a billionaire to do this.

Here are tangible ways to fulfill your success oblige by supporting others.

1. Mentor them.
2. Give them money.
3. Give them your products or services.
4. Buy their products or services.
5. Promote and recommend their products or services.
6. Jointly develop products, services, or programs.
7. Act as a reference.
8. Set a good example.

These eight activities should keep you busy for quite some time, if not for the rest of your life. By performing them, you will make a difference, even if only for a few individuals.

Wisdom

True success isn't just about what you achieve—it's about how you use those achievements to lift others up. MacKenzie Scott demonstrates that real impact comes from removing bureaucratic barriers and simply trusting good people to do good work, proving that whether you have billions or just experience to share, the obligation to help others should drive your actions.

Nordstrom's Tires

In 1975, a sixteen-year-old Nordstrom employee named Craig Trounce refunded a customer $25 because the customer was unhappy with tires he had purchased.

This story is legendary because the customer purchased the tires from the former occupant of the building. Nordstrom had taken over the location, but it did not sell him the tires. Despite this, Trounce decided to do whatever it took to make the customer happy.

This story is more compelling than any quantitative "customer satisfaction score" or marketing campaign. This illustrates how a good story is a powerful tool for remarkable people and organizations.

Wisdom

The most powerful customer service stories aren't crafted in marketing meetings—they're born when employees are empowered to do the right thing, even when it defies logic. Craig Trounce didn't just process a refund that day; he created a legacy that would define Nordstrom's commitment to customer service for decades to come.

Extras Special

Lin-Manuel Miranda is an actor, playwright, singer, and composer. He created and starred in *Hamilton* and *In the Heights*. He has won three Tony Awards, three Grammy Awards, an Emmy Award, and a MacArthur fellowship. No doubt he's remarkable.

Jon M. Chu, the director and screenwriter of *Crazy Rich Asians* and *In the Heights* (and also a remarkable person) told me

Salvation

this story about working with Miranda on the film version of *In the Heights*.

> We had a meeting for extras in the neighborhood. I never go to extras gatherings.
>
> They gather extras. They take pictures. They put them on a wall. I go there, they precut them. I go into a room full of hundreds of pictures, and I pick the type of whatever environment I want the school to be in or the environment that I want this scene to be in.
>
> So I never go to the place where they take the picture.
>
> He called me and asked, "Where are they doing that?" I said, "Oh, down the street at the theater." And he said, "I'm going."
>
> He goes there and makes a speech to these people of how much this means to him, how much this means to the community, how much he appreciates them.
>
> That's the sign of a true leader. Took time out of Lin-Manuel Miranda's day, which is a packed, full day . . . he doesn't have time for anything. He'll make it for his neighborhood.

Wisdom

Never underestimate the power of showing up in person. Lin-Manuel Miranda's presence at the extras casting, despite his packed schedule, demonstrated respect for his community and appreciation for their involvement. And Jon M. Chu's bringing it up in our interview show's Jon's awareness of showing up in person.

140 Wiser Guy

Lin-Manuel was aware that his personal interactions would have an impact, and they did. Your presence communicates that you care and are invested in the process, thereby strengthening relationships and establishing trust.

How to Keep Score

Another Jon M. Chu story. When I asked him how he measures his success, he told me by the quality of roles actors in his films get in the future.

Wisdom means rising above basing your self-worth on money, power, and fame. How you keep score says a lot about you, so here are some areas to examine to ensure you're on the right path:

Impact: Sal Khan, creator of Khan Academy, told me he cares about how many kids he's helped educate around the world. Remarkable people keep score by how much they've improved the world, not how much money or power they've accumulated.

Fulfillment: This means you love what you do, and you do what you love. Whatever the activity, it fills you with energy and provides reason for living. You feel like you've done something noble and good.

Relationships: One measure of success is the quality of your relationships. Hopefully, you've brought joy into the lives of others, and they have brought joy into yours. In short, you love and are loved.

Growth: Over the course of your lifetime you can measure your success by how much knowledge and skills you've gained. This means that expanding your horizons is a satisfying thing. This can even apply to learning to surf.

Salvation 141

> **Resilience:** You're probably successful if you can persevere in the face of challenges and failure. In other words, when you were tested, did you pass? And can you pass more tests in the future? If so, you can declare victory.
>
> **Contentment:** This means that you don't long for more of anything—except maybe time with your family and friends. Contentment indicates that you've realized what's truly important in life.

People who keep score this way are almost always gracious. If you keep score this way, you will become gracious too. The people who keep score with money, power, and fame are seldom gracious. They see everyone as a means to their end.

Your life comes down to your legacy, and how you keep score determines your legacy. I hope you made people's lives better. I hope the world is better for you having lived in it. These are the kind of legacies that matter and what remarkable people pursue.

Wisdom

Your true scorecard isn't measured in dollars, followers, or fancy titles—it's measured in lives changed, relationships strengthened, and personal growth achieved. Want to know if you're winning at life? Stop counting your bank deposits and start counting the number of people whose lives are better because you showed up, stepped up, and lifted them up.

Guy the Yard Man

You can learn as much about a person from what they ignore as from what they prioritize. And the more people ignore stuff, the more time and energy they have to devote to what is essential.

142 Wiser Guy

With all due respect to Socrates, John Locke, and Thomas Gray, all of whom are cited as possible sources of the saying "Ignorance is bliss," but the ability to ignore the small stuff is even better. That is, "ignoring is bliss."

Here's a personal example. In 1994, I was living in San Francisco with my wife and baby boy. Our house was a block from the Presidio in an expensive, mostly white neighborhood.

One day I was outside our house trimming the bougainvillea plant, and an older white woman came up to me and asked, "Do you do lawns too?" I retorted, "Because I'm Japanese, you assumed I'm the gardener, right?"

A few weeks later my father visited me, and I told him the story. I expected him to get agitated and annoyed that she assumed that his educated, author, former Apple executive son was the yardman.

Instead, he said, "Statistically, where you live, she was probably right, so don't get upset and make yourself crazy." Believe it or not, that was a pivotal moment in my life because it taught me not to look for trouble and to give people the benefit of the doubt.

Wisdom

So much of life is uncontrollable. However, we can choose our reactions and responses. If you want to be remarkable, take the high road, give people the benefit of the doubt, and use each opportunity to foster greater understanding and communication. That is, don't do what I did. . . .

Here are the on-ramps to the high road:

First, don't take things personally. If Apple has a policy that pisses you off, don't think that Tim Cook singled you out.

Salvation 143

He has no idea who you or I am. And the lady who asked
me if I did lawns wasn't necessarily trying to belittle me.

Second, don't worry about something you cannot do anything about. If you can't do anything about a situation, let
it go. For example, United delayed your flight to de-ice
your plane's wings. What will yelling at the employees at
the gate accomplish? Plus, you'll be a lot more delayed if
the plane crashes because of extra weight.

Third, give people the benefit of the doubt. Almost all the
time, people are diligent, competent, and doing their job.
A good way to go through life is assuming that people are
good until proven bad. In fact, I'd give them two or three
strikes before drawing any conclusions.

Ignoring the small stuff can also be satisfying because you're
in control and you know what's not getting to you, and it can be
good for your reputation because counterattacking (and its temporary high) will not impress anyone.

However, I mentioned the story of my neighbor in my
2022 interview with Frederick Joseph, the Black activist and
author of *The Black Friend* and *Patriarchy Blues*. Much had happened by then in terms of race relations since the woman asked
me if did lawns and my father told me to chill.

Here's what Frederick said I should have done:

> In that specific situation, a real dialogue being had about
> "what you did was problematic X, Y, and Z, and you could
> say whatever you want, but if I were a white guy doing the
> exact same thing, I highly doubt that you would." That con-
> versation might change her more than jumping down
> her throat.

144   Wiser Guy

Which is to say that I could have taken the opportunity to explain that what she said could be construed as racist and demeaning. This would combine giving her the benefit of the doubt and using the encounter as an opportunity for enlightenment.

The Honorable Steve Case

Back in the late 1980s America Online began life as Applelink Personal Edition, an Apple-labeled online service for consumers that Apple contracted Quantum to create. However, Apple blew up this contract for unknown reasons—if nothing else, this proved that Apple wasn't omniscient, as AOL went on to become a massive success.

On the day that Apple ended the Quantum Computer Services relationship in 1989, I had dinner with Steve Case, the founder of Quantum, and his team. They were in a state of shock and down in the dumps. But I told them that Apple's decision could be the best thing that ever happened to them, because they were now free to create an independent company and get off Apple's teats.

Out of desperation more than anything else, Case asked me if I would do some consulting and online conferences for $2,000 a month plus stock options. I agreed, and for the next few months I helped out, until my contact at AOL stopped asking for assistance.

I saw Case several years later, and he asked me if AOL was still paying me and had given me options. I told him that I hadn't done much work, so the company wasn't paying me, and I had never gotten the stock. I told him to "forget about it."

Nonetheless, he insisted that I get the stock, and so I received options for 2,000 shares. The stock split several times and the per-share price rose like a rocket, so these options became my

Salvation 145

version of the proverbial two fish and five loaves of bread in the Bible.

To put this into perspective, I made approximately $250,000 from Apple stock over my career. So I could make the case that the company I did the most work for provided the least money, and the company that I did the least work for provided the most.

The only reason that I made any money from AOL stock is that Case was an honorable person; he did not have to grant me those options. There was no legal paperwork that proved that he had offered them to me.

Wisdom

True success often comes disguised as setbacks, and integrity isn't about what you're legally required to do—it's about doing what's right even when no one is watching. Steve Case's decision to honor a verbal agreement years later didn't just demonstrate character; it proved that karma in business is real and sometimes pays dividends you never expected.

Honor in business isn't about contracts and legal obligations—it's about doing what's right simply because it's right. A formal contract with a dishonorable person is worth less than an informal contract with an honorable one.

Dyslexia for Dummies

My son Nate is dyslexic. If you're not familiar with the condition, here is a description of people with dyslexia:

> A dyslexic person of good or average intelligence perceives his environment in a different way, and his attention diminishes when confronted by letters or numbers. Due to a deficiency in his partial performances, his perception of these

146   Wiser Guy

> symbols differs from that by non-dyslexic people. This results
> in difficulties when learning to read, write, and do arithmetic.
> (Dr. Astrid Kopp-Duller, 1995)

Nate's school conducted open houses during which parents could go through exercises that simulated dyslexia. One exercise, for example, involved reading text that was reversed by a mirror. I couldn't complete any of the exercises—not even close. I cried after the meeting because this was the first time I understood what it was like to have dyslexia. The issue was not laziness or lack of focus.

Wisdom

Develop empathy. As the saying goes, walk a mile in the shoes of others before you judge them. If you believe overcoming learning issues like dyslexia and ADHD is simply a matter of trying harder and focusing more, you're not even close to understanding, much less empathizing.

The flip side also applies. That is, if someone isn't supportive, perhaps the person isn't evil, bad, or uncaring. Maybe this person simply doesn't know what you're going through, and you should help them walk a mile in your shoes. The open house at Nate's school was one of the most powerful experiences in my life.

It Could Be Worse

Ménière's disease is a combination of hearing loss, tinnitus (ringing in the ear), and vertigo. I have had it since approximately 1993. There is no cure for the disease as of 2018. The medical treatment is a shotgun approach:

- Reduce intake of salt, caffeine, and alcohol.
- Reduce water retention by taking a diuretic such as Dyazide.

Salvation

- Reduce stress (as if you can easily choose to experience less stress).
- Take anti-anxiety drugs such as Lorazepam.

The theory is that salt, caffeine, alcohol, stress, and anxiety might cause Ménière's. I have a different theory: My Ménière's is a result of listening to hundreds of crappy pitches from entrepreneurs. They all promised curve-jumping, patent-pending, first-mover, scalable, unicorn companies.

After more than twenty-five years of dealing with Ménière's by early 2022 I was almost completely deaf. Until my cochlear implant was activated in September of that year, I depended on live transcription to conduct podcast interviews. Live transcription wasn't great back then, so it was a struggle to be my usual conversational self.

During this period, I needed a hero to get past this handicap, and one thought kept me going: If Beethoven could compose music while deaf, then I could record podcasts by reading live transcriptions while deaf—not that I'm anywhere near Beethoven in talent.

Wisdom

Ménière's and deafness taught me many things. First, be thankful. As I write this book, Ménière's is the worst ailment that has affected me. Steve Jobs and his family would gladly have traded pancreatic cancer for a little hearing loss, tinnitus, and vertigo.

Second, look for good news. There is no known cure for Ménière's and my kind of deafness, but I'm convinced that the treatments I did for it have extended my life. I haven't added salt to food in decades. I seldom drink any alcohol. (Caffeine, however, I haven't reduced.) I take Dyazide every day, so my blood pressure is at the level of a teenager's.

148   Wiser Guy

Third, be thankful. There isn't a cure for my deafness but a cochlear implant can take you from being deaf to having lousy hearing. And believe me, this is a miracle, so I am thankful for cochlear implants and that I don't have lethal medical condition.

Fourth, be patient. There is no known cure, but someday there will be. No amount of money or social media followers can buy me the solution before it's found. For a long time, this was frustrating for a Silicon Valley guy who believed that everything has a cause, and therefore everything must have a cure, to accept.

A Dinner in Berlin

In October 2016, I went to Berlin to speak to the marketing staff of Mercedes-Benz. The night before my speech I had dinner with two German friends, and the conversation inevitably turned to the presidential election in the United States. At this point, thirty days before the election, few people believed Donald Trump would win.

The very fact that Trump was one of the two leading candidates astounded us. My friends told me that they still didn't understand how their grandparents' generation could let Adolf Hitler come to power, and they saw direct parallels between Hitler and Trump.

They warned me, "If Trump wins, it will be 1933 for America." What they meant was that before Hitler was Hitler, he was "just" a popular politician. He didn't start killing Jewish people and invading countries on his first day as chancellor.

This conversation had a profound effect on me. I didn't want my grandchildren to wonder if I resisted Trump, so I started using my social media accounts to #resist him. Few, if any, social media influencers took such an aggressive stance at the time.

They didn't want to go off-topic from their usual subjects, such as food, cats, fashion, social media, or entrepreneurship,

Salvation 149

because taking such a stance might affect their brand and cause them to lose followers. But the fear of losing followers and business were not a strong enough deterrent for me to keep silent.

So I turned my Facebook, Twitter, Google+, and even LinkedIn accounts into political feeds—contrary to the wisdom of so-called social media experts. And guess what?

While a few hundred people complained about me getting political and resisting Trump, the feedback was far and away supportive. Here are two examples:

> "You are Guy Fuckin' Kawasaki. Who gives a shit about losing some followers b/c of something you write? Your power comes from your vast experience, by you being right and you being early. Don't change from those three things."

> "I'm not willing to bring politics into my LinkedIn feed but I wholeheartedly agree with you. In fact, your persistent outspoken commentary has me questioning my own unwillingness to step up."

Wisdom

Do what's right. Influence comes with a moral obligation to stand up for your principles and to help less fortunate people. This may come with personal and short-term costs—but that's what a moral obligation entails.

I may have lost a few thousand followers, but I gained tens of thousands more. Standing up for what I believe was not only the right thing to do, it also was a good marketing decision, because my brand was aligned with democracy and meritocracy. However, even if my stance had cost me followers, branding, or income, I would still have done it.

150 Wiser Guy

That is what I will tell my grandchildren.

Dealing with Dickheads

Suppose someone who is twice your age and holds a powerful political office tries to humiliate you because you took offense to his insight on who needs abortions:

> Why is it that the women with the least likelihood of getting pregnant are the ones most worried about having abortions? Nobody wants to impregnate you if you look like a thumb.

Then-congressman Matt Gaetz picked a fight with the wrong person. Her name is Olivia Julianna. She is a "Queer, Plus Size, Latina activist" in her twenties and the director of politics and government affairs for a political activist organization called Gen Z for Change.

She slaughtered Gaetz on Twitter:

> It's come to my attention that Matt Gaetz—alleged pedophile—has said that it's always the "odious . . . 5'2 350 pound" women that "nobody wants to impregnate" who rally for abortion. I'm actually 5'11. 6'4 in heels. I wear them so the small men like you are reminded of your place.

Then she turned the controversy into a fundraising effort for abortion rights that raised $2.4 million. She has become a beacon to Gen Z and is leading the transition of power to the next generation alongside others such as Malala Yousafrai, David Hogg, Greta Thunberg, and Maxwell Frost.

Meanwhile, circa 2025, Matt Gaetz is no longer in Congress, and he isn't attorney general. Furthermore, he is haunted by the bombshell House Ethics Committee report that he paid for sex with an underage girl, abused drugs, and violated House gift rules. Besides this, he's a great guy.

Wisdom

When faced with public humiliation from those in power, or anyone at all, transform their cruelty into purposeful action that helps others. Just as Olivia Julianna turned hateful comments into millions raised for abortion rights, your response to adversity can become a powerful catalyst for positive change.

9 | Joculation

A person without a sense of humor is like a wagon
without springs. It's jolted by every pebble on the road.
—Henry Ward Beecher

Joculation: the act of making jokes or being playful.

Is Your Background Black?

One morning in the fall of 2015, I met with an African American entrepreneur who told me that he had already given a company presentation and had one more in the afternoon. He asked me if I had any tips to make his presentation better.

So I asked him, "Is your background black?" And he responded, "Yeah, I'm from a multicultural family from Atlanta." I had a good laugh and then told him, "I can see that you're Black. I'm asking if the background of your *PowerPoint* slides is black."

My theory is that white text on a black background is easier to read than black text on a white background. Also, black text on a white background says, "I created a new document and started typing."

White text on a black background shows that you're a PowerPoint ninja master who knows how to create a master page and change the color of text.

Wisdom

This is the first of some damn funny stories in this chapter. They may not involve any wisdom or lesson!

The Coolest People Use Apple Stuff

In August 2016, I was in the Apple store on State Street in Santa Barbara for my son Nate's monthly repair of his iPhone screen. A guy came up to me and asked, "Are you Hawaiian?"

I responded, "No, I'm Japanese."

Then he said, "You look like Guy Kawasaki."

I responded, "I *am* Guy Kawasaki, but I'm not Hawaiian."

He introduced himself as Shaun Tomson, and the name meant nothing to me. But the Apple genius helping me asked, "Are you *the* Shaun Tomson?"

The Shaun Tomson answered in the affirmative. The Apple genius filled me in by telling me that Shaun had been a world champion surfer in the 1970s and 1980s and was one of the most famous surfers in the world.

Okay then! Tomson and I talked, and I explained how I had tried surfing a year earlier and that my two youngest children loved it. He volunteered to take us surfing while we were in Santa Barbara.

A few days later, it happened. However, even with the help of one of the greatest surfers in the world, I could not stand up on the board. Shaun said it was because the waves were too small, but I know he was being kind.

He also said that, according to surfing rules, if your hands leave the rails and you make a movement to stand, that counts as a ride. By his count, I had four rides. But really, it was zero.

Wisdom

Talk to strangers and buy stuff at Apple stores. You can meet the coolest people there. If you want to meet me by chance, I shop at the Los Gatos, California, store.

The Electric Kool-Aid Acid Attire Test

I ran into Tom Wolfe, the famous author and journalist, at the Il Fornaio restaurant in Palo Alto, California. Wolfe's works include *Bonfire of the Vanities*, *The Right Stuff*, and *The Electric Kool-Aid Acid Test*.

He was famous for his high style—characterized by a white suit, white tie, white hat, and two-tone shoes. I was never known for my high style, nor do I care if ever will be.

When I met Tom, I was in Silicon Valley business attire: jeans and T-shirt. A mutual friend later told me that Wolfe told him, "Guy must be really powerful because he dresses like a bum."

Joculation 157

Wisdom

I could drum up a lesson from this story along these lines:

Clothes don't make the evangelist—at least in Silicon Valley.

But really, it's just damn funny story, and it did not cause me to alter my attire.

The Worst College Interview Question Ever

When one of my sons was looking at colleges to apply to, we visited the University of California at Los Angeles, and we even met with one of the vice chancellors of the school.

At the end of our meeting, she asked him, "Do you have any questions about UCLA?" His response: "Do you know where the ice hockey team practices?"

OMG! After the meeting, I pounded him, "The vice chancellor of UCLA asks you if you have any questions, and your only question is where the hockey team practices?"

Perhaps the question wasn't too damaging because UCLA accepted him. But still, I wouldn't recommend such a query during a campus visit.

Wisdom

Keep calm. You can "hover" over your kids or "lawnmower" in front of them, but in the end, things will work out without your interference. You can only do so much as a parent.

But you might coach your kids about what to say when they are asked, "Do you have any questions?" in interviews.

Jolly Ranchers Trump Baseballs

We lived in Atherton, California, for approximately thirty years, and Halloween was a big deal. One of the high points was going

158 Wiser Guy

to Willie Mays's house, two blocks from ours, because he passed out baseballs.

Word got around, and many people drove in from other parts of the Bay Area to get baseballs and have a few words with him. In case you're not familiar, Willie was one of the greatest baseball players of all time: twenty-four-time All-Star selections, two-time National League Most Valuable Player, and inducted into the Baseball Hall of Fame in 1979.

It was fun to watch the awestruck dads and their kids interact with him. One year he handed a baseball to my son Noah, then approximately ten years old.

Rather than thanking him for such a valuable memento, Noah said, "But what about the Jolly Ranchers, Willie Mays?"

Hilarity ensued—even Willie and his assistant busted out.

Wisdom

Even legends like Willie Mays can be humbled by a child's innocent honesty. Sometimes the sweetest moments in life are when we set aside our reverence for status and fame and simply interact as genuine human beings.

How to Tell If Google Might Hire You

In November 2024, I interviewed Meredith Whitaker, the CEO of Signal. This is the messaging service that many consider the most secure way to communicate in a dystopian world.

She worked at Google from 2006 to 2019. Her track record there includes founding Google's Open Research Group and M-Lab, a global network measurement platform. She also organized the 2018 Google Walkout that protested various Google practices at the time.

And here's the joculation. When we were discussing how she turned from liberal arts major to Google nerd, she told me

Joculation

she knew she was getting close to being hired during the interview process. (FYI, the process back then involved ten to twelve interviews with various Google employees.)

She explained, "I knew I was getting close to getting hired because the wedding rings of the people interviewing me were getting bigger and bigger."

Wisdom

If I was to extract some wisdom out of this story it would be that Whitaker's story highlights the need to observe subtler dynamics and nuances beyond formal processes during interviews. Finding your advantage often requires an awareness of interpersonal subtleties as much as job expertise.

Or I could just tell you that this is another damn funny story—you pick.

What's $745,000 Between Friends?

In 1986, Apple had a problem: We were running out of "fans" who would buy anything from the company they loved. Unfortunately, other people weren't buying Macintoshes because they thought that there wasn't a large enough selection of software. (They were right, but we didn't let the truth get in the way of Macintosh evangelism.)

Mike Murray, the Macintosh Division's director of marketing, told me to change this perception of reality. We decided that Apple's dealers and Apple's salespeople were the right place to start to change this impression, so we had to convince them that Macintosh had lots of innovative software.

We came up with a plan to buy 1,500 copies of ten different software programs at $50 each to give them. Murray told me to execute the plan, so I contacted the ten companies and negotiated the deal. Back then software cost $200 to $500, so a

160   Wiser Guy

$50 price was a huge discount. However, because this program offered exposure to Apple's dealers and salesforce, the companies quickly agreed.

So far, so good. Everything rolled along, and while the software companies manufactured the products, I got a purchase order for $750,000 (1,500 copies × 10 programs × $50/copy). I presented the invoices to the finance department, and Susan Barnes, the vice president of finance of the Macintosh Division, went berserk. My spending limit was $5,000, so she was incensed that I had spent a mere $745,000 more than that.

Rumor had it that Jobs told her to fire me. My side of the story was that Murray, my boss, had told me to get it done, so I got it done. Fast forward to 2016. At a reunion of Macintosh Division employees, I asked Barnes about this story. She said that Steve had no intention of firing me—he just wanted her to scare the shit out of me.

I still believe that I did the right thing. If you tell some people to get something done, they will do it. Murray told me to change the perception of Macintosh lacking software, and he also told me that we had the budget, so I did what I had to do. End of story.

Wisdom

Trust, but document—especially if you're exceeding your spending limit by 150 times! It's good to cover your ass when you're bending the rules. I should have sent Murray a memo confirming that he wanted me to buy the software. Then he would have had to deal with the wrath of Jobs, not me.

Life Regresses to the Mean

An injury to my eye in 2015 required that I not wear contact lenses for several weeks, so I played hockey with glasses. The first

Joculation 161

time that I did so, I also drank a Jamaica Blue Mountain coffee from Philz—a $10 cup of Joe.

That day I scored six goals. A day later I played again, and I scored another six goals. The time after that, four goals. Then I played in a high-level game where I was the worst player and scored two goals. I had never scored as many goals before (and never would again).

I understand superstition. For example, rumor has it that Michael Jordan wore the same North Carolina shorts under his Chicago Bulls shorts for his entire career. There may have been causative reasons for my scoring streak:

- Caffeine improved my athletic performance.
- Glasses provided better vision than contacts.
- Glasses provided worse vision and fogged up, so I had to compensate by focusing more on the puck.
- There were lousy goalies for those games.

Shortly after this, even wearing glasses, I went back to seldom scoring. Scientists call this "regressing to the mean"—that is, returning to my average level of play. But the scoring streak sure was fun while it lasted.

Wisdom

Don't get cocky when things are good because you will regress to "what you really are" over the long run. Sometimes when I surf, I catch the first five waves and start to believe that I'll just catch the next twenty. Then I miss the next five.

And the flip side is also true. That is, when you're in the dumps, regression to the mean predicts that you'll do better soon. To wit, I've also had surf sessions where I miss the first five waves, and then I catch the next five.

162 Wiser Guy

The wise thing to do is to keep working so you regress to a higher, better true self.

Mutual Distrust

In 1987, I was Apple's chief evangelist, and I was in the room when Lee Clow of the advertising agency Chiat\Day presented the Think Different campaign to Steve Jobs.

There were perhaps ten marketing people in the meeting, and I remember that Lee's presentation took our breath away because it so perfectly captured the spirit of Macintosh and Apple.

At the end of the meeting, he said to Steve, "I have two copies of these ads. I'll give one to you and one to Guy."

Steve, as only Steve would, responded, "Don't give Guy a copy. Just give me a copy."

This was a man-or-mouse moment that you don't want to look back on and think, "Why did I wimp out?" So I didn't. Right then and there, in front of everyone, I came back with "Don't you trust me, Steve?"

And he came back with "I don't."

And I came back with "That's okay, Steve, because I don't trust you either." That probably cost me a few million dollars in stock options, but it was worth it.

Wisdom

Sometimes you have to seize the day and go for it. I have never regretted saying what I said. And a few years later, Steve tried to get me to come back to Apple.

Of course, I turned that down too—and that's why I still have to work and write books.

Joculation 163

WTF

Here's a quiz for you. Who was the first person to drop an F bomb on the *Remarkable People* podcast?

a. Gary Vaynerchuk
b. Steve Wozniak
c. Neil deGrasse Tyson
d. Margaret Atwood
e. Angela Duckworth

The answer, shockingly, is Margaret Atwood, the doyenne of dystopia and author of *The Handmaid's Tale*. Here's how this remarkable story came to be.

In our interview, I asked her about her research, writing, and editing process. She told me that she finds someone in real life who is similar to the character in her book and asks them to review her draft.

> I wrote a book in which the narrator was a young man with commitment issues.
>
> So I got a reader who was a young man with commitment issues to say what he thought of it. He gave me two tips.
>
> "First of all, don't say, 'What in the fuck.' Say, 'What the fuck.'" And second, he said, "That's not how you smoke a joint."

And that's how Margaret Atwood beat Gary Vaynerchuk to the punch.

Wisdom

It's not a stretch to learn to test the veracity of your writing with a "real person." That's valuable advice.

But honestly the reason why I include this story is because it is . . . So. Damn. Funny.

10 | Validation

When you see validation for a life's work and
dedication, it's a beautiful day.

—Mary Gauthier

Validation: process of confirming the accuracy, legitimacy, or
acceptability of something.

Nic Kawasaki, Son

One night in December 2017, I was back at my childhood home in Atherton. It was around ten at night, and I was getting ready to leave for an adult hockey league game in Redwood City.

Because it was late, below forty degrees outside, and most of the lights in the house had been turned off, I assumed that my family would all be asleep as I stealthily packed my hockey bag and threw it into the trunk of my car.

But right when I began to pull out of the driveway, I noticed a light on in the back of our family's minivan. I rolled over to investigate from behind the wheel of the electric car I was driving at the time and saw a figure hunched over in the driver's seat of the minivan. I was a little nervous by this point, but as I leaned over and turned a light on, I saw that it was just my dad, bent over reading something.

I asked him what he was doing, and he said he was putting something away in the car. Classic Guy Kawasaki move. I took this as one of my dad's moments when he was trying to do something small that could really wait until the morning, but had to do it right then and there, just as his father would have before him (something that my mom always teases him about).

We spoke for a few moments, and as I was getting ready to tell him good night and peel off into the dark Atherton night, my dad asked me where I was going. I told him I had a game down at the Redwood City rink, and with a look of concern and a glance down at his watch, he asked me what time.

I replied that we had the late game slot at 10:30 p.m., and he said that he might come watch. I thanked him and told him he didn't have to see his washed-up son play, sort of shrugging off his comment as a I drove down the driveway and toward the rink.

168 Wiser Guy

About thirty minutes later, at 10:15 p.m., as I was taking part in the pregame warm-up, I skated around the ice, getting the blood flowing and the wrists warmed up by firing pucks into the empty net, when one of my teammates came up to me and gave a nod toward the glass in front of the lower seating area of the ice rink.

"Did Guy come to watch us play?" He pointed over to the side of the indoor seating area behind the plexiglass that was closest to the rink entrance.

At first I didn't say anything, then I gave the guy a shove and said, "Yeah, right." But then he repeated the question and pointed again, this time with a more urgent look in his eye. So to humor him, I looked over and squinted. Holy shit, there he was.

My dad, sitting there all alone in his jeans and sweatshirt, watching me play a meaningless adult hockey league game in the middle of the night. Honestly, my first thought was, *Oh, man, Mom is going to be pissed if he's tired and groggy tomorrow.*

The first period began. I scored a couple of goals, and it felt good to show the old man that I could still skate despite being a corporate sellout. At that point I was just happy to put some pucks in the net while he was still there, and I assumed he would leave after about the first half hour or so. But when the second period ended, he was still there.

After a bit, the buzzer rang, signifying the end of the game, and I still saw him sitting in the stands. I couldn't help but be brought back to when he would come to every game I played when I was younger and then in college.

He went home after the game ended, and after drying my gear I walked in the kitchen and saw him. He complimented my game and offered a few words of encouragement as I grabbed some food and prepared to go to sleep.

It was something along the lines of "You sure can still score some goals." I smiled and said thanks, wished him a good night, and then hit the hay. But I would never forget that night.

When my dad asked me if I would like to write a chapter, I said sure. I love my dad, and he has imparted an incredible amount of wisdom to me, either intentionally or unintentionally, throughout the years up until my life now as a working adult.

However, I had no idea what I was going to write about until that night. That experience that night got me thinking about how my dad has been as a father and a man. It was that night that inspired my hindsight.

I played a lot of sports in high school. There were literally hundreds of football games, lacrosse games, and countless road trips for my ice hockey teams. My dad was always there. He once chartered a private jet so that he could speak in Detroit and still make my high school "senior" football game.

Wisdom

I know what you may be thinking: Fathers are always there for their kids when they are growing up. I agree. But I wasn't a kid that night at the rink in Redwood City. At least in my mind I wasn't anymore. I was twenty-four, I had a full-time job, and I lived in an apartment in San Francisco.

But my dad still came and watched me, even though I was a bird that had left the proverbial nest. I could see the joy in his face and feel the warmth in his voice as we chatted after the game that night while standing in our kitchen. It made me realize that even though I am technically now an adult, I will always be his son, and he will always be there for me.

Put your family before anything else. As my father has done for me and our family, I will be there for mine no matter how busy I may become, or what other obligations I may have as I get older. I also realized that no matter how old I get, when I get married or (gulp) have children, I will always be my father's son, and he will always love me like one.

Peg Fitzpatrick, Co-author

On a visit to Silicon Valley, I ran an errand with Guy to pick up photos at Walgreens. We went into the store, and Guy picked up his photos and then grabbed a gallon of milk, bread, peanut butter, and jelly.

After paying we left the store, and Guy walked over to a homeless man who was sitting off to the side of the entrance. I didn't notice him on the way in. Guy gave him all the groceries that he had purchased. He didn't make a big deal of it, and naturally the man was appreciative.

It was such a thoughtful act. Few people would think of, or take the time to do, something like this. People might not expect a selfless act from a famous speaker and author, but it's exactly the type of person that Guy is. I'd be willing to guess he doesn't even remember doing this. [Peg is right. I don't remember this at all.]

Wisdom

Help when you can, where you can. Instead of looking at the bigger picture of homelessness and not being able to solve the problem, Guy zoomed into to assist one person. It didn't take much time or much money.

It only took one person seeing another person on the street and helping. Imagine if we all did one selfless act like this a day. We need more people to think like this in our world.

Noah Kawasaki, Son

In 2017, our family bought a house in Santa Cruz. Almost immediately, my dad started meeting everyone and making connections left and right. Also, I was in the beginning of my junior year at UCLA and was beginning to think more seriously about

Validation 171

a future career path. What industry? What company? What department? I wasn't very sure.

My dad's enthusiasm for this new place had him fantasizing about me finding a great internship nearby and spending the summer living, working, and surfing in Santa Cruz. He said I would be "living the dream."

So sometime later I got a text from my dad saying that he'd found three cool companies: O'Neill, Inboard, and Looker. I already knew what O'Neill was (a surf brand). Inboard was a new electric skateboard company, which I also thought was pretty cool.

Then there was this company called Looker. It looked like this super cool, fun, and challenging new tech company in Santa Cruz. I spent a lot of time researching them on Google, watching their YouTube videos, checking out ratings on Glassdoor, and so on. The more time I spent reading about Looker, the more I knew that Looker was the one.

My dad texted me again a couple of days later and told me to rank these three companies in the order I would like to work for them. I replied with my listing, though the one that really mattered was Looker. He replied, "Hardest order," as in Looker would be the hardest one to pull off.

Fast forward a couple of months, and I had been exchanging emails with one of Looker's recruiters, having phone calls with the director of the customer support team, and having lunch in the office with my would-be managers. I don't know the exact actions my dad took to make this happen, but it was definitely swaying Looker to consider my resume.

I ended up accepting an internship offer and "living the dream" that summer in Santa Cruz. It was such an incredible experience of working, learning, making friends, being stressed out, and having fun that I accepted a full-time return offer before going back down to UCLA for senior year.

172 Wiser Guy

Because of my dad, I was able to have a worry-free senior year, got a job at a great company straight out of school, and still got to see my family every week.

Wisdom

Give your children infinite opportunities and every advantage to be successful. Support them when they want to try learning something new. Don't be afraid to ask others for favors.

Also, if you want to keep your children close, find them great jobs nearby and give them *indefinite* free rent and washer-dryer privileges.

Madisun Nuismer, Co-author and Producer

To pick a singular story about Guy has not been easy, so I have chosen to share three. Some may seem trivial, but to me they have spoken volumes.

Many of you may think Guy had to conduct thousands of interviews to find his working wing woman before he found me. That's not the case. Guy and I met in the ocean while—you may have guessed—surfing.

I got to know Guy while surfing at the same local break as him. He was a similar face during dawn patrol sessions. He always dropped in on me, but I couldn't get mad because of how joyful he looked on waves. One random day, just after he finished burning me badly on a set wave, he got to talking to me about his podcast, and how he was about to interview Dr. Leana Wen, CNN's leading public health expert.

The waves were in my favor that day because I had gotten my bachelor's degree in public health, and when I shared that with Guy, he asked for my help in writing questions for her interview and doing background research.

Validation 173

Ten hours of random work for Guy turned into a full-time job. He has become more than a boss to me, but a dear friend. He must have been happy with my initial work—or just felt bad for how many times he dropped in on me.

In all seriousness, Guy took a chance on me and decided to invest in me. He had faith in my abilities and made me a part of his projects and daily life. In the end, both of us benefited and our lives changed for the better.

The second story is not much of a story, but it will give you insight into Guy as a boss and friend. My family is from the Midwest, and whenever they visit me in Santa Cruz, Guy is adamant about meeting whoever is visiting and taking us to lunch. (Guy has a very busy schedule, and people would pay lots of money to have lunch with him.)

He does it because he genuinely cares about me, and wants to understand where I came from and show interest in my family. This means the world to me, and has made Guy feel like family to me, too. It would be impossible to have him solely as my boss. He is also a mentor and "uncle."

The last story takes place in summer 2023. I went to Indonesia for a month to travel and surf. When I originally proposed it to Guy, he was fully supportive. However, he showed a father-like concern for my safety and before I left, he had me stop by his house to give me something (we are neighbors.)

Guy placed in my hand two AirTags for my two pieces of luggage—one for my fanny pack, and one for my backpack stuffed with all my belongings for the next month. He made sure they were already activated, and not only that, but he paired both to his phone so that he would be the first to know where I was if I got kidnapped or my luggage got stolen. Safe to say I felt protected the next month in Indonesia.

And the funny thing is that I left one of the AirTags in Denpasar, and it hasn't moved in two years if you want to get it for us.

174 Wiser Guy

Wisdom

I've learned much from Guy:

> First, life's most meaningful connections often arise from serendipitous moments, as long as we remain open to recognizing and nurturing the potential in unexpected encounters. And we look beyond the breach in etiquette of dropping in on you in the water.
>
> Second, the truest leaders understand that investing time in knowing their people's roots and stories is far more valuable than any business meeting. When someone consistently makes space in their life to honor what matters most to you, they become woven into the fabric of your life.

Last but not least, life's most meaningful gifts often come wrapped not in grand gestures, but in simple acts of genuine care and forethought like two AirTags. True friendship is built brick by brick over the course of time.

Shawn Welch, Co-author

We first met in February 2012 when Guy was writing *What the Plus!* and needed help converting bullet points from Microsoft Word to the Kindle Direct Publishing (KDP) platform. I responded to his public plea for help (on Google+) and sent an email offering my assistance.

To my surprise, Guy sent me his entire manuscript almost immediately and outlined the problems he was having. He had no idea who I was or what my background was. He only knew I said I could help.

That evening I converted a chapter and sent it back to him, along with a picture of his book on my Kindle. If you haven't learned it by now, Guy is a very much a "show, don't tell" person. Show the magic first, then explain what you did.

Validation   175

I'm not sure what I expected, but it certainly wasn't what happened. After some back and forth over the next couple of days Guy asked me to lay out and produce *What the Plus!* and for the next four months we worked side by side launching that book.

Then that summer we were having coffee in Palo Alto and decided others would benefit from what we had learned together, so we decided to co-author *APE: Author, Publisher, Entrepreneur.*

How I met Guy is not unique; it's a pattern with how Guy finds and works with new people. I've seen Guy hire unproven copywriters, cover designers, social media consultants, and more. Guy looks for competence, not a resume.

He isn't afraid to admit what he doesn't know, and he surrounds himself with people who not only fill in the gaps but also have their own spark to bring to the table.

Wisdom

First, admit when you don't know something and don't be afraid to seek out help. Don't think that you're above learning from someone else.

Second, look for competence, not a resume. Don't be afraid to give unproven people a chance.

But Wait, Shawn Has More

When Guy originally asked me to contribute to this book I was honored. I consider him a true friend and wrote what I felt was an honest depiction of the story you just read. He cut more than half of it. And the parts the he cut were the nice things I said about him.

Guy might fly first class and share stories of nice cars and big trips. But when it comes to the way he carries himself as a person, he is the first to decline a compliment. He is humble in his abilities, and quick to give credit to others.

176 Wiser Guy

I'm adding this back in on my second edit (let's see if he cuts it a second time) because I think there's some important wisdom there as well.

More Wisdom

Be humble, be relational. Nobody gets where they are without the help of others in one way or another. Be quick to reward those who helped you along the way. Focus on amicable relationships and genuinely work to help others succeed without the thought of a quid pro quo.

Nate Kawasaki, Son

My dad once asked me what he could do to improve as a father. I had no idea what to say then, and honestly, I still don't. Instead of answering that question, I think it's better to share some of the lessons he's taught me over the years. These little moments stick with me, like chapters in a book, but the numbers of each chapter represent my age during the time of the event.

This one starts with Chapter 10, "You're Not Stupid."

"Well good morning, Fernando! Good morning, Greg! We hope you guys are having a great day in this lovely weather!" The radio's cheerful voice echoed through the car as my dad drove me to school. It was middle school, specifically for kids with dyslexia.

I hated going—not just because I had to sit in a classroom and do work, but because reading was a big part of everything. My ten-year-old self didn't think reading mattered much. I figured I could get by without it in my world.

My parents knew I had dyslexia. I knew it too. But instead of seeing it as just another challenge, I saw it as something wrong with me—something that made me less human, less normal.

Validation 177

Even in the Charles Armstrong School, full of kids like me, I felt out of place.

As we got close to the school entrance, my dad turned the radio down and looked at me. "Your teachers are telling me you're spelling your sentences backwards or flipping them. Do you think you're doing that?"

I felt a lump rise in my throat. I couldn't look at him. "Yeah," I muttered, turning toward the window. "But it's fine. I know I'm stupid."

The words stung as I said them, but I believed them. "I know I'm different. It's because I'm stupid," I added, clenching my mouth so hard my throat hurt as I held back tears.

My dad slowed the car down and looked at me. His voice was firm, yet full of care. "You are not stupid. Don't ever tell yourself that you're stupid." He paused, his gaze strong. "Don't let anyone make you believe you're less than them because of what you haven't learned yet. Don't let them put you in a box or a category. You are you. You might have a harder time with some things, but everyone has challenges they face in life."

He took a deep breath and continued. "Or maybe . . . maybe you just haven't been taught the right way yet."

That conversation marked the beginning of a long journey for me—the journey of learning to let go of the idea that I was "stupid." It wasn't an overnight change. The thought still came back at times, creeping into my mind during difficult moments in my educational life.

But my dad—and my mom—kept reminding me. They wouldn't let me forget that I wasn't defined by my struggles. My dad always told me I'd get through it. "It might take longer than it does for others," he'd say, "but no matter what, you've just gotta keep pushing forward."

Next is Chapter 15, "Don't Mistake Aloha for Weakness"

178   Wiser Guy

Growing up, I've always watched my dad interact with people in a way that was so full of energy. There was always laughter, and sometimes animated hand gestures. Or if he had pen and paper, there were notes about the conversation for the person. It didn't matter if he'd known someone for years or had just met them—he made every conversation seem like it mattered. But I'd sometimes wonder: Was he really enjoying it? Or was it a mask, hiding how he actually felt?

From the outside, it always seemed like he was having a good time. Still, I'd debate whether I should play the role of "rescuer" and give him an out with a classic shirt tug and a line like "I'm hungry, let's go," or "Dad, Mom wants you home." But honestly, anyone who knows Pidgin would just laugh and say, "Brah, da guy like talk story."

My dad is the kind of person who would head back to the car and say, "Nate, grab the Merge4 socks out of the car. Let's give those to the people I was just talking to." His actions taught me that kindness and respect go a long way because you never know what someone's going through. He's shown me that if you can support someone, you should.

It wasn't just his friends he cared about. He'd ask about my friends, too—checking in, offering rides home, or even making breakfast for kids who weren't his own. Sometimes I'd think, man, this kid isn't even your son, and here you are making him breakfast for the third morning in a row. And yet, without realizing it, I've started to mirror his behavior. One summer, I think I had eight kids staying over at the house.

Usually, my dad would say hi to everyone, then either head out to surf or jump into a meeting. But this time he hung back, waited until everyone left, and called me downstairs. "Nate, let me talk to you," he said.

I ran downstairs. "What's up?"

He looked at me seriously. "Are those all your boys?"

Without hesitation, I replied, "Yeah."

He nodded but got straight to the point. "Nate, don't be taken advantage of."

I was caught off guard. "Dad, they're my friends. I think I'm good."

He nodded again, agreeing but making his message clear. "I have a lot of friends too. I love having parties and bringing people together, but I also know one thing—I don't let people take advantage of me. Don't let anyone fuck you over. I don't want that to happen to you."

He paused for a moment, then continued. "I love that you have friends, and I love that you're there for people. I'm not saying these kids are taking advantage of you. I'm just saying it can happen. I love that you offer to help others when they need it, but just remember—some people might see that as an opportunity to take advantage."

At the time, I wasn't prepared for that conversation. I hadn't thought about it like that before. But I'm grateful my dad said it.

And then there's Chapter 17, "Don't Bullshit a Bullshitter"

Everyone has lied at some point—it's just one of those unfortunate truths about being human. Whether it's to avoid trouble, dodge responsibility, or just make life easier in the moment, we've all done it. At seventeen, I had mastered the art of quick responses to questions like "Did you do your homework? Did you clean your room? Your car? The front yard? Did you pick up the clothes?"

Without fail, my answer was always "yes," whether it was true or not. And without fail, my dad would immediately hit me with his now-famous line: "Nate, don't bullshit a bullshitter."

The first time he said it, I was caught off guard. I thought, *What the hell does that even mean?* It didn't fully sink in for me, so

180 Wiser Guy

I kept making excuses like "I forgot," or "You never told me," even though, deep down, I knew better.

These weren't things a parent should have to constantly remind me about—they should've been instinctive actions on my part.

And yet, my dad still found ways to hold me accountable, when he'd occasionally send me photo evidence of my room at home—usually a pile of clothes on the ground—with a simple text: "You can't say you didn't see this."

But even as I kept up my charade, claiming I had done whatever chore or avoided whatever trouble, his words started to stick. Whether I was lying about picking up clothes or denying that I'd trespassed somewhere I probably shouldn't have been, my dad always knew.

One night, after a particularly long string of these conversations, my dad sat me down at dinner. "Nate," he said, "why the fuck are you lying? Why don't you just do it now rather than later?"

I laughed it off, but something about his tone told me this was different. That night, I decided to ask him straight up: "Dad, what the fuck does 'Don't bullshit a bullshitter' even mean?" My mom spit out her drink and started laughing.

He leaned back in his chair, grinned, and said, "It means you shouldn't try to deceive, lie, or manipulate someone who's experienced or skilled at spotting dishonesty—because they'll see right through it. I've been there, done that, and I know the game better than you do."

It was like he dropped the mic right there at the dinner table. I thought, *Whoa, my dad just spit some real bars.* And honestly? He wasn't wrong. I'd come to realize there was no point in lying to him—he always saw right through it.

Since then, I've been straight up with him, even if it sometimes got me into trouble. He always tried to understand where I was coming from, giving me the space to figure out for myself whether I was right or wrong. This brought us closer because I knew my dad was someone I could be honest with and turn to whenever I was feeling down.

Now, I can't wait to use this line on my own kids one day. Looking back, reading and writing moments like these remind me that my dad didn't need to ask how to be a better father—he was already doing it.

Wisdom

Lots to digest here. First, real leadership starts with heart. Never let others define your limitations or capabilities. The strongest leaders understand that challenges aren't deficits—they're just different paths to success. Sometimes people simply haven't found the right way to learn yet.

Second, practice radical aloha, but keep your spine. Genuine kindness and generosity are superpowers, not weaknesses. Being welcoming and supportive doesn't mean being a pushover. Build community and show care, but maintain clear boundaries. Those who truly understand aloha know it's about strength as much as warmth.

Third, cut the crap; build trust instead. Authenticity beats clever deception every time. When you're straight with people, they become straight with you. Trust isn't built through convenient lies or dodging responsibility—it's earned through consistent truth-telling, even when it's uncomfortable. The best relationships are founded on honest communication.

Scott Knaster, Macintosh Developer Support

In 1986, I was manager of technical support for developers. Guy gave me a nontechnical assignment. He had met the physicist for the Grateful Dead—go back and read that again if you need to—and asked me to set up a private concert at Apple with the Grateful Dead. For no money. Maybe I could give them a Mac.

The most popular touring band in the history of rock and roll, who had played in front of more than twenty-five million people, and I was supposed to get them to come to Apple and play a show for free, because they were interested in the Mac.

I tried. It didn't exactly work out. Instead of a free concert, we got Bob Weir, John Perry Barlow, and I think Mickey Hart, to give a private talk for us in an Apple building on DeAnza Boulevard—not what we had imagined, but as the saying goes, "You have to aim for the stars if you want to hit the clock tower."

In case you're wondering, Steve wasn't there. This was during his exile from Apple.

At the event, Barlow said they had written a song on the Mac we had given them, but the Mac crashed, and they lost the song. But then he said that didn't really happen. He made it up! He couldn't stay with the lie though, because "It's bad karma to lie to Deadheads. Lying to Deadheads about this would be like drowning puppies."

Wisdom

There's much to garner from this adventure, First, Guy's chutzpah knows no bounds. Who else would even think to ask the most popular touring band to give a free concert in exchange for one Macintosh? And it sort of worked.

Second, success isn't about "settling." You've got to recognize and embrace alternate forms of victory. In this case, getting these legends to appear for us at private talk was huge.

Third, John Perry Barlow's fessing up is a great lesson in respecting the power of karma. Lying to your fans and true believers is an insanely stupid thing to do.

Fourth, give people opportunities that are outside their areas of experience. I was pretty good at supporting developers, and I guess Guy trusted me, so he made me a concert promoter. Guy is great at providing bold opportunities for others around him.

Rebecca Hoover, Educational Therapist

It is the beginning of December and it is clear to me that the situation in a ceramics class is dire. This course is required for the major of one of Guy's kids, but the campus ceramics studio is closed for the holidays. The student hasn't started the final project. There are days left until the end-of-semester party and the final assessment.

And then Guy, who happened to be visiting the campus over Thanksgiving break, gets a full debrief on his son's predicament. No final project? No studio time available? No hope for passing the class? No problem. There is always a way.

Within twenty-four hours, I am receiving pictures of bowls and cups being churned out at a local studio that Guy had called after an online search for "ceramic studios near me." More importantly, I get a call from a very relieved student who is not only feeling hopeful again, but who is now getting the opportunity to show just how talented he is.

But it doesn't stop there. The professor offers extra credit for making food for the end-of-semester party. But you live in a dorm and don't have a baking pan and whisk . . . no problem. Guy and his son make butter mochi in his hotel room after a run to the local market.

While Guy is on campus, he notices that the art department is having a Christmas craft fair and is looking for volunteers. Guess who he "volunteers" to further integrate into the art

184

Wiser Guy

department community. And finally, ten handblown glass cups, also due in a few days for another class, are possible.

Wisdom

In addition to being an evangelist, author, and speaker, Guy can also now add educational therapist to his job portfolio. I know this because I am one, and I have seen firsthand how transformative it can be when a struggling student has someone's attention.

This story is not about getting an A in a college ceramics course, although I was thrilled that things worked out that way, and it certainly isn't about rescuing a struggling student by doing his work, because Guy has zero artistic talent.

It is about teaching that student how to hold onto hope, even when everything turns to shit, figuring out a way, and seizing the opportunity to shine. And it is about parents being active in their kid's education and showing their love with tangible actions.

Nohemi Kawaski, Daughter

Every summer for about eighteen years, my family spent one to two weeks at the Family Vacation Center (FVC) on the campus of UC Santa Barbara. This is a family camp where kids have fun activities with their counselors while their parents explore Santa Barbara, taste wine, ride bikes, and surf.

In August 2011, I was excited to be going to camp. It was an event I looked forward to all year, and I had two super-close friends who were attending the same week as our family, so we could all hang out.

At that time, I was overly obsessed with the well-known pop star Justin Bieber. My dad fully supported this. In fact, he'd taken me and my girlfriends to two Justin Bieber concerts. I collected

Validation

about ten foldout posters of the singer from *Pop Star*, my go-to magazine, and I brought the posters with me to camp.

Each family had a space with bedrooms for the kids and bedrooms for the parents. Of course, I loved decorating my side of the room that I shared with my younger brother, so I took the opportunity to hang them all up the second I got settled in.

A couple of days went by and as I was hanging with the other kids in my group, I decided to share my excitement about my posters. Moments later, one of the other girls said something along the lines of "Why did you bring Justin Bieber posters to camp?" and "You're, like, so obsessed with him." I was traumatized.

Being a person who tends to hold her emotions inside, I just smiled with a neutral expression, and I probably responded, "I just really like him," and went on with the day. But the second we got released from group, I went to our building and ran right into my room and ripped all of the posters off the wall.

I cried. I was so hurt.

With anger and sadness, I smashed the posters into a ball, threw them in the trash, and ran straight to my dad. While crying hysterically, with tears running down my face, I told him what had happened. He gave me a big hug and told me everything would be okay and how sorry he was.

I told him I had to meet my kids' group for evening activities, so he wiped the tears off my face, gave me a big kiss on the head, and I left for the gathering. When I came back that night, still upset from what had happened earlier that day, I threw off my shoes and went straight into my room.

I discovered that my dad had rehung up each and every one of my posters on the wall. While I was gone, he had taken each poster out of the trash, unraveled them, taped them back together, then put them back up. I was at a loss for words. My dad felt so bad for me.

Wisdom

My dad didn't want other girls to influence me. He wanted me to be proud of my posters and ignore what the other girls had said. Looking at the posters, I smiled, and knew in that moment how much my dad loved me.

It's a cruel world we live in, and we would be lying if we said we have never been met with a bully or someone who chose to say something just to make us feel like crap. Yeah, my dad could have given me a kiss, said everything will be okay, and moved on. But it was his act of putting all my posters back up on my wall that stuck with me.

When I walked into that room, at that moment, I knew my dad had my back. So have your kids' back too. Pick them up when they get knocked down. Not every time, because they need to build some resilience for the world we live in. But sometimes. From this I learned that your parents' words and advice are important, but it's their actions that stick with you forever.

Summation

[A] quotation is a handy thing to have about, saving
one the trouble of thinking for oneself, always a
laborious business.

—A. A. Milne

Summation: A comprehensive summary or recapitulation of
previously stated facts or statements.

As we wrap up this journey through the twists and turns of my
life, I hope you've gleaned some wisdom from my experiences,
both the triumphs and the face-plants.

Looking back, my life wasn't a straight line. It was more like
a long surfing adventure:

- Pick a beach: law, medicine, dentistry, tech, etc.
- Pick a break: hardware, software, etc.
- Pick a wave: Apple, Amiga, Commodore, IBM, etc.

Things get interesting at the wave level:

- When do you start paddling?
- What direction should you paddle?

188 Summation

- Who else is on the wave?
- When do you pop up?
- When do you turn?
- When do you get off?

What was the point of this surfing metaphor? Good question. Not much. I just like to use surfing metaphors. But here's what you may be able to learn from my life.

The Power of Perspective

Remember when I almost became a doctor? Life has a funny way of steering us away from paths that aren't meant for us. Sometimes, it takes fainting in a hospital to realize you're not cut out for medicine. Other times, it's a stern Army officer teaching you to respect authority over a clump of rice. The point is, every experience, no matter how small or seemingly insignificant, shapes who we become.

You Never Know

Exciting opportunities often come disguised as detours. Who would have thought that meeting another car-loving teenager at Stanford would lead to a career at Apple? Or that a sixth-grade teacher's advice would alter the entire trajectory of my life? The lesson here is clear: Stay open to possibilities, even when they don't fit your plan.

Hard Work and High Standards

It is profoundly important to subject yourself to people who challenge you. Harold Keables didn't just teach me English composition; he instilled in me a lifelong commitment to excellence. Those grammar exercises weren't just about semicolons and serial commas—they were about holding yourself to a higher standard in everything you do.

Steve Jobs didn't just teach me how to sell computers. He instilled in me a lifelong commitment to good user experience, elegance, and mission-driven assholatry.

Comfort Zones Are for Wimps

Leaving Hawaii for California was like stepping into a whole new world. It was terrifying, exhilarating, and absolutely necessary for my growth. Don't be afraid to take that leap into the unknown.

Whether it's moving across the country for college or trying your hand at a new industry, growth happens outside your comfort zone. And moving from Hawaii to California was nothing compared to my great-grandparents moving from Japan to Hawaii.

Importance of Gratitude

If there's one regret I have, it's not thanking Trudy Akau and Harold Keables before it was too late. So let me say this loud and clear: Express your gratitude to those who've helped you along the way. You never know when a simple "thank you" might make all the difference in someone's life. And you never know when a person's time is up, and you won't get to express your gratitude.

Final Thoughts

Your journey will be unique, and there's no one-size-fits-all formula for success. Sometimes you'll make the right choices, and sometimes you'll screw up royally. But if you stay curious, work hard, and remain open to new possibilities, you'll find your way.

190   Summation

And, if all else fails, remember that at least you didn't faint on your first hospital tour, turn down the CEO position of Yahoo!, quit the most valuable company in the world twice, and tell Steve Jobs that you didn't trust him. On the other hand, you may start the next Canva.

Now go out there and write your own story. Who knows? Maybe one day you'll pen a book about your wild ride. Just make sure to use proper grammar—Harold Keables and I expect nothing less.

About the Authors

Guy Kawasaki is the chief evangelist of Canva, host of the *Remarkable People* podcast, author of *Think Remarkable* and sixteen other books, and adjunct professor of UC Santa Cruz. He was the chief evangelist of Apple, trustee of the Wikimedia Foundation, and brand ambassador of Mercedes-Benz. Kawasaki has a BA from Stanford University, an MBA from UCLA, and an honorary doctorate from Babson College.

Madisun Nuismer is the producer of the *Remarkable People* podcast and co-author of *Think Remarkable*. Nuismer has a BA in public health from the University of Nebraska at Omaha. She also attended the Institute of Integrative Nutrition and is a certified holistic health coach.

Index

100 Foot Wave (TV series), 55

A

Aaker, David, 121–122

A/B testing, 51

Accomplishment, 56

ACIUS, launch, 81

ADHD, learning issue, 146

Advantage, finding, 159

Agenda, setting, 54

Akau, Trudy
(impact), 4–5, 189

Aloha, practice, 181

Amazon, success (working
backward), 120–121

American Dream,
epitomization, 38

Amyotrophic lateral
sclerosis (ALS), 35

Analogic perspective
taking, 91–92

AOL, success, 144

*APE: Author, Publisher,
Entrepreneur* (Kawasaki/
Welch), 175

Apology
analysis, 83–84
process, learning, 84–85

Apple
failures, impact, 43
fan problem, 159–160
products, functionality
(increase), 126
Quantum Computer
Services, relationship
(cessation), 144
resignation, 81
Think Different campaign,
Chiat/Day presentation,
162
work, quality, 47

Apple University Consortium,
running, 102–103

Artist's Way, The (Cameron), 25

Index

Art of Social Media, The
(Kawasaki/
Fitzpatrick), 105
Artonomics, launch, 37
Ask Group, launch, 23
Assumptions, challenge, 123
Atwater, Ann, 57
Atwood, Margaret, 163
Authenticity, 136
benefit, 181
Azril, Ade Harmusa, 69–70

B

Balwani, Sonny (con-
viction), 78
Barlow, John Perry, 182
Barnes, Susan, 160
Basquiat, Jean Michel, 37
Beliefs, support, 149
Benefit of the doubt, 142–144
Benioff, Marc, 75–76
Bertish, Chris, 124
Bieber, Justin, 184–185
Big data, usage, 51
Black Friend, The (Joseph), 143
Boich, Mike, 11, 19, 76, 89
job offerings, 101–103
Boldness
regrets, 71
success, 53
Bonds, fostering, 62
Bonfire of the Vanities
(Wolfe), 156
Bonobos, sales
problem, 68–69

Boss, communication, 80
Branding, 121–122
Branson, Richard, 50
Bravery, importance, 36
Brick-and-mortar store,
advantage, 69
Broughall, Steve, 111–113
Brown, Jack, 52–54
Bryar, Colin, 120
*Build: An Unorthodox Guide to
Making Things Worth
Making* (Faddell), 126
Bureaucracy, issues, 111
Bystander effect, 98

C

Cameron, Julia, 25
Canva
initiation, 40–41
job offer/acceptance,
process, 105–107
Career
decisions, 11–13
job offer avoid-
ance, 103–105
molding, 68
Caring, importance, 173
Case, Steve, 144–145
Chabris, Chris, 66, 93
Chain reaction, impact, 89
Challenge, preparation
method, 59
Chances, taking (impact), 72
Change
embracing, 99–100

Index

empathy, impact, 92
power, 49, 99–100
value, 85–86
Chan, Jackie, 22
Character, test, 60
Charles Armstrong
  School, 177
Chicago Manual of Style, The
  (reading), 8
Children
  father support,
    167–169, 186
  home, exit, 169
  honesty, impact, 158
  hovering/lawn-
    mowering, 157
Choice, power, 36
Chu, Jon M., 138–141
Cialdini, Bob, 61
Clothes, impact (potential),
  156–157
Clow, Lee, 162
Coach, search, 50
Cochlear implant,
  usage, 147–148
Cohen, Geoffrey, 91–92
Collective knowledge,
  harnessing, 96
College interview
  question, example,
  157
Comfort zone
  avoidance, 189
  exit, 4
Commonality, search, 54–55

Communication, fostering,
  142
Community service, ded-
  ication, 14
Compassion
  conscious action, equiv-
    alence, 119
  fostering, 62, 92
Competence, test, 60
Competition, estimation,
  101
Complaints, 24–25
Complementary people,
  power (harness-
    ing), 95–96
Complementary skills, lev-
  eraging, 96
Compliment, declining, 175
Concept, proof, 123–125
Confessions of a Chauffeur
  (Webster), 135
Connections
  building, 103
  fostering, 54
  happiness, link, 62
  missed connections,
    impact, 72
  regrets, 71–72
  source, 174
Contentment, exami-
  nation, 141
Controlling assholes, 127
Cook, Tim, 142–143
Courage, importance, 43
Crazy Rich Asians (Chu), 138

196 Index

Creation, imagination
(transition), 123–125
Creativity, molding, 68
Criticism, impact, 25
Curiosity, embracing, 123
Customer
happiness, 138
role, 117
satisfaction score, 138
service, quality, 42
Cynicism, conversion, 26

D
Deafness, 147–148
Decision-making, 77–78
importance, 110
deGrasse Tyson, Neil, 109, 163
Delbourg-Delphis,
Maryléne, 81–82
Demand/supply curves,
intersection, 57–58
Depression, 35
Details, ignoring
(benefit), 142
Determination, value, 66
Detours, opportunity
disguise, 188
Dickheads, handling, 150–151
Digital Research, Apple
(lawsuit),
52–53
Discernment, power
(development), 67
Dishonesty
denunciation, 79

detection, 180
Disney, Walt (job loss), 44
Divides, bridging, 57
Donations, 136–137
"Do Schools Kill Creativity?"
(Robinson), 124
Doubt
benefit of the
doubt, 142–144
compartmentalization, 25
conversion, 26
Duckworth, Angela, 163
Dweck, Carol, 48, 135–136
Dyslexia, 145–146,
176–177
learning issue, 146

E
eBay, founding, 57–58
Ebert, Dave, 95–96
Edu-Ware Services, job
offering
(decline), 102–103
Ego-driven assholes, 127
*Electric Kool-Aid Acid Test,
The* (Wolfe),
156
Ellis, C.P., 56–57
Emotions, containment, 185
Empathy
action, 119
development/fostering,
54, 62, 146
expression, 84
impact, 92

Index

Employee recruitment/ retention, motivational tools, 47

Enchantment (Kawasaki), 69

Energy, channeling, 62

Environment, perception (differences), 145–146

Excellence, commitment, 188–189

Experiences
learning, 7
positivity, 21–22
power, 149
wisdom, 187

Experts, believing, 122–123

F

Facebook, political feeds, 149

Faddell, Tony, 126–128

Failure
forgiveness, 111
opportunities, 74
regret, 72
success derivation, 27
transformation, 44
value, 43–44

Family Vacation Center (FVC), 184

Fauci, Tony (interview), 13–15

Fear
facing/confrontation, 43, 56
impact, 6–7

Feldhaus, Dan (impact), 9

Fitzpatrick, Peg, 105–107, 170

Fixed mindset, problem, 48–49

Flowers, blooming (metaphor), 130–131

Flowers, Halim (prison/ opportunities), 36–37

Foster, Joe, 26
white space, 121

Foundation regrets, 71

Fraud, denunciation, 79

Frey, Sarah, 42–43

Frost, Maxwell, 160

Fulfillment, examination, 140

Fusion Books, launch, 40

G

Gaetz, Matt
argument, loss, 150–151
House Ethics Committee report, 151

Gassée, Jean-Louise, 80–82

Gates, Bill (success), 66, 74

Genchi genbutsu (go and see for yourself), Toyota principle, 117–118

Genovese, Kitty (Genovese effect), 97

Goodall, Jane, 123
friendship, 89
interview, 34
opportunities, 34–35

Good situations, concept, 91

Goods, pricing market (creation), 57–58

198   Index

Good Writing: An Informal Manual of Style (Vrooman), 8
Google+, political feeds, 149
Google Walkout, Whitaker organization, 158
Grandin, Temple, 118–119
Graphical environment manager (GEM), issue, 52–53
Gratitude
  expression, 5
  importance, 189
Gray, Thomas, 142
"Great Hanoi Rat Hunt: A Conversation with Michael G. Vann" (Vann/Clarke), 60
Grit, importance, 49
Growth, examination, 140
Growth mindset
  embracing, 135–136
  opportunity, 48–49, 86
Gruber, Marty, 51

H
Hamilton (Miranda), 138
Hand gestures, animation, 178
Handmaid's Tale, The (Atwood), 163
Haoles (derogatory term), 4
Happiness/connections, link, 62
Hardass, role, 8–9
Harding, Wanda, 85–86

Hardship, conversion, 37
Hard work, importance, 49, 188–189
Hart, Mickey, 182
Harvard Study of Adult Development, 61–62
Hearing loss, 146
Helping, value, 76, 170
Hewlett, Bill, 31–32
Hewlett-Packard
  launch, 31
  technology revolution, 32
High standards, importance, 188–189
Hitler, Adolf (Trump, parallels), 148
Hockey scores, causative reasons, 161
Hogg, David, 150
Holmes, Elizabeth (conviction), 78
Homeless man, Guy donation, 170
Hometown, exit, 11
Honest opinion, expression (consideration), 93–94
Honesty
  competence/character test, 60
  impact, 158
  sense, 5
Honor, sense, 5
Hoover, Rebecca, 183–184
Hope, retention, 184
Humility, 175–176

Index

I

If You Want to Write (Ueland), 32–33, 48

Ignorance, 110–111

"Ignorance is bliss," 142

Imagination, transition, 123–125

Impact, examination, 140

Improvement
importance, 24–25
speeches, impact, 71

Incentives/objectives, alignment (ensuring), 61

Indispensability, importance, 39–40

Influence, source/moral obligation, 149

Inner compass, attention, 79

Inner critic, facing, 25–26

Inner demotivator, cessation, 25

Inner life, development, 37

Innovation, 110
accidents, impact, 73–75
"creating what you want to use" method, 117
understanding, correlation, 119

In-person appearance, power, 139

Intellectual property, transgression, 53

Internships, 39

Interventions, 91

Interview, preparation method, 59

In the Heights (Miranda/ Chu), 138–139

Invisible gorilla experiment, 92–93

Iolani private school, attendance, 4, 7–9

J

Job
candidates, acceptability (determination), 101–103
quitting, considerations, 82

Jobs, Steve, 5, 32, 50
employee firing, 160
excellence, demands, 60
interactions, 47
meeting, 59
mistrust, 190
motivation, 20–21
mutual distrust, 162
pancreatic cancer, 147
performative mastery, 108–109
reality distortion, 90–91
success, 66, 74
Wozniak, impact, 95

Joculation, 158–159

Jordan, Michael (shorts, wearing), 161

Joseph, Frederick, 143

Julianna, Olivia (argument, win), 150–151

200 Index

K

Kalihi Elementary
  attendance, 4, 6
  detention, 7
Karma, power (respect), 182
Kasalow, Jordan, 119
Kato, Russell, 12
Kawasaki, Guy
  Apple firing, 160
  caring, importance, 173
  chutzpah, 182
  compliment, declining, 175
  educational thera-
    pist, role, 184
  Grateful Dead appreciation,
    181–182
  hiring practice, 175
  homeless man,
    donation, 170
  humility, 175
  lessons, 174
  patrol sessions, 172
  volunteering, 183–184
Kawasaki, Nate, 176–181
  bullshitting, 179–180
  charade, 180
  dyslexia, 176–177
  intelligence, father
    affirmation, 177
  message, 179
  understanding, 180–181
Kawasaki, Nic
  hockey game, father
    observation, 167–169
  pregame warm-up, 168

Kawasaki, Noah, 170–172
  career, 171
  company ranking, 171–172
Kawasaki, Nohemi, 184–186
  emotions, containment,
    185
  Guy, emotions (feeling),
    185
Keables, Harold (impact),
    8, 188–189
Khan, Sal, 140
Kitschke, Zach, 106
Knaster, Scott, 181–183
Knoware, criticism, 59–60
Knowledge, absence
    (admission), 175
Known, resistance, 11
Kodak (failure), working
    backward
    (absence), 120–121
Kovalcski, Serge, 82–83
Ku Klux Klan, membership
    (renunciation), 57
Kurtzig, Sandy, 23

L

Langer, Elizabeth, 77
Laughter, presence, 178, 180
Law of big numbers,
    128–130
Leadership
  focus, requirement, 128
  heart, importance, 181
Lead generation, 69
Leakey, Louis, 35–36

Index

Learning
  issues, overcoming
    (difficulty), 146
  value, 66
Leopold, Lisa (apology,
  review), 83–84
Lieberman, Mike, 102
Life
  inner life, development, 37
  lesson, 59
  regression, 160–162
  regrets, timidity/missed
    connections (impact),
    72
  trajectory, 188
  winning, 3
Lindstrom, Martin, 118
LinkedIn
  commonalities, 55
  political feeds, 149
Locke, John, 142
Lythcott-Haims, Julie, 109

M
Macintosh
  computers, usage, 90–91
  evangelism, 159
Macintosh Way, The (Kawasaki),
  33, 81–82
Magic, display, 174
Man-or-mouse moment,
  162
Manson, Mark, 72–73
Mao Zedong, 130
Martinez, Jacob, 136–137

*Math Mind: The Simple Path to
  Loving Math*
  (Sharma), 96
Mayall, Will, 81
Mays, Willie, 158
McGill, Archie, 59
McNamara, Garrett
  (successes), 55–56
Mean, regression, 160–162
Ménière's disease, cure
  (absence), 146–147
Mentors, impact, 36, 39, 137
Mindfulness, 77
*Mindset: The New Psychology of
  Success* (Dweck), 48
Miranda, Lin-
  Manuel, 138–140
Mission-driven asshole,
  role, 126–128
Mistakes, opportunities, 74
Moke (derogatory term),
  21
Moral obligation, 149
Moral regrets, 72
Morals, shaping, 5–6
Moritz, Michael,
  103–104
Motivation
  forms, 19–20
  impact, 26–27
  importance, 22
  source, 20–21
Murray, Mike, 159–160
Musk, Elon, 94
Mutual distrust, 162

Index

N

Natural ability, preparation (contrast), 59

Negative experience, change, 78–79

Negative feedback, absence, 32

Negative response, generalization (avoidance), 41

Nesmith Graham, Bette, 117

Niche
creation, 122
ownership, 39

Niño, Martha (perseverance), 37–38

No decision, transformation, 41

Non-degreed people, hiring, 65

Nudges, embracing, 99–100

Nuismer, Madisun, 95, 172–174
hiring, 65–66, 173

Numeracy, absence (problems), 97

O

Obama, Barack, 10, 50

Obama, Michelle, 109–110

Obrecht, Cliff, 40, 106

Off-the-books learning/ benefit, 26

Omidyar, Pierre, 57–58

Open architecture, 125–126

Open-ended questions, asking, 92

Opinions, validity (affirmation), 91

Opportunities
disguise, 188
seizing, 35, 74

Other Side: From a Shack to Silicon Valley (Niño), 38

Overdelivery, importance, 42

Ownership, taking, 84

P

Packard, David, 31–32

Packard, Julie (interview), 31–32

Pain, alleviation, 117

Passion
source, 73
unveiling, 111–113

Passivity, avoidance, 3

Patience, handling, 52

Patriarchy Blues (Joseph), 143

Peet, Andrea Lytle, 35–36

People
assistance, 4–5
complementary people, power (harnessing), 95–96
influence, 5–6
leader, time investment, 174
values/morals, shaping, 5–6

Perception, differences, 145–146

Perfection, hope, 78

Index

Performative actions, 109
Performative, beauty,
    107–109
Perkins, Melanie, 106
  Obrecht/Adams, impact,
    95
  rejection, over-
    coming, 40–41
Personal discovery, path
    (creation), 123
Personal growth,
    achievement, 141
Personal risk, 79
Perspective
  embracing, 123
  power, 188
Persuasion, importance,
    54
Pink, Daniel, 71–72
Political assholes, 127
Political feeds, conversion
    (feedback), 149149
Possibilities, openness,
    189–190
Power of Regrets, The (Pink),
    71
Principles, support (moral
    obligation), 149
Products/services, creation,
    125–126
Proverbial nest, children
    (exit), 169
Punching down, problems,
    82–83
Purpose, source, 73

Q

Questioning, power, 123
Quicken, usage, 23
Quitting, decision
    (bravery), 13

R

Race relations, 143
Reality, perception
    (change), 159–160
Reebok, white space, 121
Regrets, types, 71–72
Rejection
  enduring, 52
  overcoming, 41
Relationships
  building, 54
  examination, 140
  strengthening, 141
  value, 103
Remarkable People podcast,
    F word (usage), 163
Remorse, absence, 84
Resilience, 36, 130
  building, 186
  examination, 141
Responsibility, dodging,
    181
Rewriting, 72–73
Ribardière, Laurent, 81
Right Stuff, The (Wolfe),
    156
Rober, Mark, 85–86
Robinson, Ken, 123–125
Role models, impact, 14

204 Index

Rometty, Ginni
 (non-degreed people, hiring), 65–66
Russo-Japanese War, 3

S
Sacrifice, requirement, 328
Salesforce.com, starting/success, 75–76
Sales, obtaining, 69
Schultz, Tyler
 (decision-making, importance), 78–79
Scott, MacKenzie (donations), 136–137
Sculley, John, 81
Search-engine optimization, 51
Self-doubt, impact, 49
Self-esteem, loss, 21
Self-flattery, avoidance, 22
Self-overestimation, avoidance, 101
Selling process, learning, 51–52
Sequoia Capital, 104–105
Shared goals, focus, 57
Shared story, listening, 92
Sharma, Shalinee, 96–97
Sherrell, Paul (apology), 83–85
Simons, Dan, 93
Sino-Japanese War, 3
Sivers, Derek, 89–91
 opportunities, 67–68

TED Talk, 89–90
Skills
 college degrees, contrast, 66
 complementary skills, leveraging, 96
Skill set, expansion, 39
Social media
 accounts, 69–70, 148–149
 chatter, ignoring, 111
Social pressure, 61
Societal norms, bending, 110
Socrates, 142
Solo dancer, attraction, 90
Spielberg, Steven (USC rejection), 44
Standards, setting, 39
Stanford University
 attendance, 9–10
 path, decision, 11–13
Stories, value, 58
Strategic decision-making, importance, 110
Strength, sign, 100–101
Subcategory, creation (difficulty), 122
Subtle Art of Not Giving a F*ck: A Counterintuitive Approach to Living a Good Life (Manson), 72
Success
 causative reasons, 161
 derivation, 27
 disguise, 145
 fear, facing, 43
 inspiration, embracing, 23

Index

meaning, 137
price, payment, 70–71
production, skills
  (impact), 66
Success oblige, 137
Superstition, under-
  standing, 161

T

Taiken gakushuu (experiential
  learning), 118
Teachers, enjoyment/
  investment, 85–86
Tenacity, requirement, 38
Test, preparation method, 59
Thaler, Richard, 99
Think Different campaign,
  Chiat/Day presen-
  tation, 162
Thunberg, Greta, 150
Time, leader investment,
  174
Timidity, impact, 72
Tinnitus, 146
Tomson, Shaun, 155–156
Transgressions
  impact, 5–6
  justification, 84
Trounce, Craig, 138
True character, revealing,
  136
Trump, Donald
  Hitler, parallels, 148
  punching down incident,
  82

resistance, 148–149
Trump Reich, 149
Trust, 160, 183
  absence, 162
  earning, 52
  importance, 42
  mutual distrust, 162
Twitter, political feeds, 149

U

UC Davis, attendance/exit, 12
UCLA, attendance, 51
Ueland, Brenda, 32, 48
Uncertainty, 130
  harnessing, 78
Understanding
  fostering, 92, 142
  innovation, correlation, 119
  source, 118
Unexpected jobs/gigs,
  embracing, 68
Unfamiliarity, overcoming, 54
Universe, denting, 5, 48
Unknown, embracing, 11

V

Values
  shaping, 5–6
  source, 15
Vaynerchuk, Gary, 163
Vision, 130
Vrooman, Alan, 8
Vulnerability
  display, issue, 100–101
  transformation, 56

206 Index

W
Weakness, display, 100–101
Webster, Chris, 135
Weir, Bob, 182
Welch, Shawn, 174–176
Wen, Leana, 172
What the Plus! (Kawa-
saki), 174–175
Whitaker, Meredith, 158–159
Google Walkout, 158
White space (Reebok), 121
White text/black background
(PowerPoint slide
effectiveness), 155
Widman-Levy, Ronit, 89
Winfrey, Oprah (job loss), 44
Wisdom, 187
meaning, 140
Wise interventions,
concept, 91
Wolfe, Tom, 156–157
Working backward, 120–121
World Regret Project, 71–72

Wozniak, Steve, 20,
32, 117, 163
success, 74
Writing
inspiration, 33
steps, 72–73
Writing, veracity (test), 163

Y
Yamaguchi, Kristi, 27
Yamaguchi, Roy, 41
Yocam, Del, 79–81
Yousafrai, Malala, 150

Z
Zatoichi, weakness/strength
example, 100
Zetsche, Dieter, 68, 94
Zimmern, Andrew
indispensability, 39–40
overdelivery, 41–42
Zuckerberg, Mark, 117
success, 66

ALSO FROM
GUY KAWASAKI
MADISUN NUISMER

Think Remarkable • ISBN: 978-1-394-24522-2

WILEY